The Best Kept Secret in YWAM!

D0564773

The
Best Kept
Secret in
YWAM

The Gleanings Miracle:
A Miraculous Story
of Justice and Mercy for the Hungry

Steve Witmer

HARMON
PRESS

The Best Kept Secret in YWAM. The Gleanings Miracle: A
Miraculous Story of Justice and Mercy for the Hungry

Published by
Harmon Press
Woodinville, WA 98077
http://www.harmonpress.com

ISBN-10: 0-9799076-1-6
ISBN-13: 978-0-9799076-1-6

Library of Congress Control Number: 2008931938

All Scripture quotations, unless otherwise noted, are taken from
The New International Version of the Bible, © 1975, 1978, 1984 by
International Bible Society.

Cover design by: Blue Z Studios, www.bluezstudios.com

Contents

Acknowledgements 1

Foreword 5

Introduction 7

1. The Story Begins 9

2. Humble Beginnings 15

3. Cuyama: A True Veggie Tale............................23

4. Bikes and Pledges: Racing Toward the Future 29

5. Dedication Day: June 11, 1989 43

6. Touching The World with the Fruit of Gleanings 47

7. Maturing of the Ministry...................................57

8. Oh, How the Mighty Have Fallen.......................63

9. From Death, New Life 75

   A Photographic Journey 87

10. A Miracle of Mercy 99

11. The Unfinished Story......................................107

Appendix

1. Ministries Page..111

2. Product Donation 127

3. Charities Watchdog..137

4. Angel Story 141

5. Testimonies..149

About the Author...163

ACKNOWLEDGEMENTS

The remarkable story of Gleanings has been called "the best kept secret in Youth With A Mission." The telling of the story has required regular pauses for reflection and thanksgiving for the Father's vision and wisdom. Many were the hands and hearts that took that vision and daily fleshed it out through their sacrificial service. They are the true heroes of this story.

There are hundreds of individuals deserving of special recognition on these pages; although time and space has not allowed for this. I am confident that a far greater volume is being written in heaven where each deserving Gleanings' servant will receive the Father's affirmation.

This project would not have been possible without the vision and assistance of several key friends and leaders. Their encouragement kept me on track and have ensured the accuracy of the finished product. To each of you I am very thankful!

Wally and Norma Wenge, you modeled the love of Christ to me through your faith and compassion for the hungry. You have shaped my life and "ruined me for the ordinary." Wally, although you have finished your earthly ministry, your dream lives on, and is now being carried in the hearts of thousands. You have been a true leader and, to many a spiritual Father. I am one of your sons in the faith. Thank you!

The Gleanings' staff, past and present, are worthy of double honor. For the countless hours you've served and the piles of research materials you assembled, I am most grateful. Len and Lois, Rick and Lynn, Ralph and Linda, Ron and Shirley, and Dave and Candi, you are all champions! May the loving Father grant you the rewards you greatly deserve.

Doug and Ellie, you have walked the journey with me, sharing the same experiences and working side by side at Gleanings (how many times did we etch our names in freshly poured concrete?) Doug you've been mentor, coach, and (at times) cheerleader. Thank you!

Charity and Cheryth, you are amazing! You've taken pages of handwritten text, deciphered it (a miracle in itself!) and produced the finished work we see today. Gord, I am forever indebted to your masterful skills in polishing the finished product. You are a true servant, my friend!

To my brothers, Doug and Barry, thank you for the years you've helped to organize bus loads of volunteers to serve at Gleanings. You've taken vacation time to work extremely hard, demonstrating in unmistakable ways your compassion for the poor. You are more than biological brothers; you are my co-laborers in ministry. Deserving much more than an honorable mention, I'm confident that your rich reward awaits in heaven.

To my church families at Wellspring Christian Center and Bible Fellowship, your loving acceptance and affirmation has given me the courage to continue. Thank you.

How can I thank God adequately for my family? Becky, you have loved me unconditionally for thirty-two years. Your patience with this project was commendable, giving up valuable vacation time, we poured over journals and freshly written lines. Our tears fell onto pages filled with personal memories. Thank you for embarking on this amazingly rewarding and unpredictable life of service. To our children, Heather and Shannon, the tree house I built for you in 1987 is no longer visible at Gleanings, but every time I glance at that tree I imagine you playing there. Where have the years gone? You have grown into extraordinary young women and mothers. Johnny and Justin, thank you for having the courage to join our family and for loving our daughters. Together, you have all been a quiet source of strength, memories, and inspiration in our attempt to capture the Gleanings story. Thank you!

Steve Witmer
Surrey, BC
2008

FOREWORD

BY DOUGLAS A. HAGEY

My dear friend, Steve Witmer, writes from his personal passion for missions and mercy ministries. He is not documenting these events as an observer or spectator, but as one of the participants in the unfolding story. For years, he has walked the pathway the Master modeled — showing acts of mercy and kindness. As a pastor, he leads his congregation out of the box and into the world.

The Gleanings story is one that *should* be told. It is centered in a man who *should* be remembered — a man with a huge vision and a matching heart of compassion. It is the account of a remarkable journey of faith in response to God's concern for the hungry. Its foundation is justice and mercy. It is a chronicle of adventure and sacrifice, of the amazingly creative use of once-wasted resources, of the involvement of thousands of people from around the globe, each captivated by their own unique understanding of the vision. It is a tale of a "good-news" gospel that alleviates the physical human suffering of tens of thousands, while offering spiritual hope for a better future.

The book you hold in your hands is much more than a documentary of the birth of a ministry – It is the story of a journey of faith into uncharted territory. Let it stretch you into finding new ways to participate in caring for the world's hungry and hurting.

Douglas A. Hagey
Friend of Gleanings
Teacher
Author of *In Search of the Church*

INTRODUCTION

I first met Wally Wenge in 1986. His disarming laughter and friendly personality quickly drew me into friendship. However, it was more than Wally's personality; it was his passion that most impacted me. To that point in my life, I had never witnessed a leader so captivated by the needs of the poor that he was moved to tears — every time he talked about them!

This was authentic leadership; Christlike in quality. For Wally and Norma Wenge, it was not a hardship to divest their life of privilege to become advocates for the needy, it was their greatest joy. As they emptied themselves, God flooded in to meet their every need.

That is the Gleanings miracle…

I was given a front row seat to this glorious story. My life was impacted and in many ways, it was ruined for the ordinary, by the ministry of Gleanings for the Hungry. This good news story, one that has been a best kept secret, must be told. It is a story of God's faithfulness and God's provision. This saga continues, and there are more chapters to be written, but this one thing is certain: God will receive all glory and honor! After all, this story was His idea in the first place, and He deserves all the credit.

As you read on, I trust you will look beyond the faithful workers (these are the characters in our story) to the Author Himself. Notice the fingerprints of God on every detail as He expertly guided and directed this great work. So, perhaps this is not our story, but rather it is His story. After all, He has called himself, "the Father to the fatherless…" and the "defender of the poor and oppressed."

My prayer is that you will be inspired as you read the Gleanings story. However, more essential than inspiration is my desire that you be motivated to action, that you would be challenged to reflect God's heart by meeting needs around you or around the world. Together let us carry the compassionate love of the Father to those that need it most.

Wally and Norma Wenge did, and the multitudes are forever grateful.

CHAPTER 1
THE STORY BEGINS

Forget the former things; do not dwell on the past.
See I am doing a new thing, do you not perceive it? Isaiah 43.18–19

The UN bus slowly wound its way through the Thai countryside. Passing government checkpoints it eventually came to a stop just two or three miles inside Cambodia. Although the situation was still tense in 1981, the Thai government was actively closing down the Cambodian refugee camps and resettling the Cambodians in their own country.

Wally Wenge and his wife Norma had been chosen to lead the repatriation of this bus filled with refugees. Most of them were here against their will; they feared for their lives and the safety of their children. The jungles were littered with land mines and provided cover for the lingering remnants of Pol Pot's loyalists.

The drop-off point was a remote area of jungle. From this lonely place these refugees would blend into the jungle, seeking safety, and hopefully reunite with family members who were driven from their homes in villages and towns. An estimated 500,000 thousand were killed during this horrific season in Cambodia's history. For these disembarking passengers, the memories were still too vivid and the wounds yet unhealed.

On this sultry day, Wally, Norma, and others were handing out UN food rations to each one. There was a mixture of emotions expressed on these beautiful faces: gratitude, fear, anxiety, and tears.

Urgently and tearfully a young Cambodian woman approached Wally. In her arms lay her child, wrapped only in a soiled blanket. With a broken heart, which only a mother can understand, she insistently attempted to give Wally her child. She was barely more than a child herself, just a teenager, and yet, like all mothers wanted the best for her child. The child was likely the product of a rape by a Thai soldier "guarding" the refugee camp. Instinctively the mother knew that her infant faced not only physical hardship in the devastated countryside, but also very likely rejection by her own village.

That single encounter played a pivotal role in the lives of Wally and Norma Wenge. The young mother's desperate cry and the plight of her young child remained vivid in their hearts and minds. Years later, they would recount this incident "as if it were yesterday," and the compassionate tears would overflow. God had captured their hearts for the needy, or perhaps it was that God had given them a touch of His Father's heart for the people he had created. That day became a defining moment, the launching of a life and ministry dedicated to "the least of these...."

God had shown the Wenges the desperate need; now he would call them to service in a unique way. It was December 1981 and Wally and Norma were visiting their daughter Coleen in Sacramento, California, for the Christmas holiday. Wally, ever the early riser, was alone in the early morning, relaxing, and playing a game. Suddenly, he heard the Lord speak into his heart, "Wally, get your diary, I want to talk to you." Moments later, the Lord firmly repeated His command and Wally responded. Some time before in Thailand, during his personal devotional time, Wally had read in Leviticus 19.9–10 and Deuteronomy 24.19–22 that the Israelite farmers were not to harvest to the edge of their fields, rather they were to leave the perimeter, the "gleanings" for the widow, orphan, alien, and poor. Wally posed the musing question to the Lord: What are the gleanings today that are to be used to care for the underprivileged? Now, months later, the Lord showed Wally that the gleanings of California were the tons of cull fruit, which were being thrown away annually. This nutritious food was discarded because of its size, color, or shape, and was allowed to rot between the perfectly spaced trees in the San Joaquin Valley orchards.

Excitedly, Wally shared his new insights with Norma. She told of having read the passage in Ruth chapter 2 where the alien Ruth was given favor in the fields of Boaz as she gleaned alongside the harvesters. Could it be that the Lord would show favor to them as they "gleaned on behalf of the poor?"

Excited and overwhelmed by the scope of this endeavor, Wally called his good friend, the President and founder of YWAM: Loren Cunningham. Wally served alongside Loren as a member of YWAM's International Council and had become a trusted co-laborer, carrying much responsibility in YWAM's rapid growth and expansion, from the international headquarters at Kona, Hawaii.

Listening intently to Wally's remarkable story, Loren blessed and lovingly released him to pursue God's call. It is what Loren shared next that perhaps best captured God's "plan for His man:" Wally Wenge. Reminding him of the installation ceremony in March 1975, at the North America Staff Conference in New Jersey where Wally had been appointed to YWAM's International Council, Loren made note of three specific prayers. Joy Dawson, Paul Hawkins, and Loren had each prayed prophetically that Wally would have a "Joseph" style of ministry. Wally tells the story in his journal:

> While being prayed for by the International Council, March of 1975, (the council consisted of Loren Cunningham, Don Stephens, Floyd McClung, Jim Rogers, and Jim Dawson) Don Stephens had a prophecy that the Lord would give me a "Joseph Ministry." At the same time, Loren got the scripture in Genesis on

Joseph. Others prayed and then Loren asked the YWAM staff if any of them had anything. Paul Hawkins stood up and gave the same scriptures in Genesis on Joseph. Paul and I were rooming together and he told me later that the power of God was so strong on him that he had to "hang on the table to keep from falling." Although this message was veiled at that time, it was now becoming clear.

Taking leave of his administration duties for YWAM Kona, Wally and Norma took simple faith-filled steps of obedience. Armed with a God-sized vision and hearts bursting with compassion, they joined countless others who had gone before them saying: "Lord, here I am, send me." Thus with these simple words began the great journey of faith and adventure, a ministry we now call Gleanings for the Hungry!

CHAPTER 2
HUMBLE BEGINNINGS

Suppose a brother or sister is without clothes or daily food.
If one of you says to him, "Go, I wish you well; keep warm and
well fed, but does nothing about his physical needs, what good is it?
In the same way, faith by itself, if not accompanied by action, is dead.
James 2.15–17

Convinced that God was calling them to an adventure in mercy ministries, Wally and Norma began to pursue goals and make contacts within the California Central Valley agriculture community. Sovereignly, God began to connect them with old friends and new acquaintances that provided valuable insights. Over the years Wally would marvel at the exquisite timing of the Lord in supplying the needed provision at the perfect time.

Following his Christmas encounter with the Lord in 1981, Wally and Norma traveled to Fresno, California, in the Central Valley staying with friends Floyd and

Ida Watson. As Wally shared passionately of his vision to glean the valley's fruit to feed the needy, Floyd and Ida's hearts were stirred to participate in this budding faith adventure. Floyd offered to introduce Wally to some of his good friends in the orchard, fruit packing, and dehydration businesses. These simple introductions would become the nucleus of a new ministry: Gleanings for the Hungry!

Wally was first introduced to Don Jackson, a farmer and orchardist and Wayne Adams, the manager of Sunworld Fruits. Upon hearing the need, they were stirred to participate as well. Pledging to donate and transport cull peaches and nectarines, these men became the first of many growers and packers who generously donated millions of pounds of fresh fruit annually.

Having secured the initial supply of fruit, there was still the issue of where to set up the processing and how to actually dehydrate the product. Wally, by his own admission, stated that he hated kitchen duties and knew nothing about food! Years later, Wally would comically concede that when Gleanings began, what he knew about fruit dehydration "could fit into a thimble — with room to spare for your finger!" Again, God had the right person and a facility prepared. Wayne Adams introduced Wally to Dale Sedoo who owned a raisin dehydration facility in Yettem, California. Dale offered his dehydrator for six weeks in the summer (his off-season). This was to be the seasonal home of Gleanings for the Hungry for the next five years. Dale's expertise in drying fruit provided the knowledge and foundation to begin this new ministry.

The pieces were falling into place. Wally had fruit promised, a facility provided, and a basic understanding of how to get started. All this God had supplied, yet Wally had no cash reserves for operational costs. Floyd Watson, hearing of Wally's progress asked, "How much money do you have, Wally?" Responding with his ever-hearty laugh and contagious faith, Wally shared that although he had no money, he knew a great big and faithful God! Floyd and Ida gave $2,000.

It seemed that Father God noticed each area of Norma and Wally's need before they asked. The ministry required a dependable vehicle, one that could handle the valley heat and shuttle the early volunteers. Len and Lois Nylin, childhood friends of Wally, felt impressed to purchase a Mazda Sedan and ten months of insurance. God's provision again! As need after need was met, it became obviously apparent that God's blessing and confirmation was upon Gleanings.

With promising vision they forged ahead, undaunted by the Herculean task that awaited them. The summer of 1982 was one of trial and discovery. Using the spartan Yettem facility, they began the labor-intensive method of handling each peach individually. Wally had been given a simple piece of machinery. One peach at a time was inserted, the foot pedal was pressed and the peach was cut in half! The halved fruit was placed on borrowed raisin trays (3' x 5') and placed in the sun to dry. The hot California sun performed its magic and dehydration was completed in three to four days. As the fruit dried they noticed it turned dark. The rich natural sugars darkened in the heat. Although perfectly nutritious and palatable, it was not esthetically pleasing, so starting in 1982 the fruit was treated with sulfur dioxide, a color preservative used in the preparation of some dried fruits.

In the first few years, the volunteer staff were primarily local folks from a community church called Wellspring Christian Center. The pastor, Doug Hagey, himself a former YWAM-er, became ready friends with the Wenges and supported their efforts with regular assistance. The Hageys, Ayers, Peacocks, Schmidts, Neffs, and many others would donate a day here or there to ease the workload. While the team busied themselves with preparing the fruit, Norma would slip away to the small travel trailer (which served as the Wenge's lodging) and hastily prepare lunch for whoever had showed up for the days work!

The second full season of fruit dehydration was 1983. Wally strategically recruited young YWAM staff to assist in the fruit processing. Three came from Salem Oregon: David Rue, Don Kaufer, and David Romero. From Hawaii came a young Burmese student called Osberg, John Davidson from YWAM Los Angeles, and Diane Thompson rounded out the YWAM team.

Diane Williams was perhaps the most enthusiastic and energetic of all the summer volunteers. Through their fellowship, Wellspring Christian Center, Willie and Diane Williams learned of the Gleanings initiative. Diane visited and soon became a regular! Her boundless compassion had previously caused her to become involved with the local youth authority facility, a low-security jail for troubled youth. Through her contacts, Diane negotiated "day passes" for young offenders to serve at the Yettem facility. What remarkable, godly passion and prayers surrounded those young men on a regular basis! Additionally, Willie and Diane would house the workers who would arrive from out of the immediate area, providing much needed hospitality.

The summer of 1981 indeed was a season of discovery. There was so much to learn, friendships to be forged, and momentum to be gained. That year the total production was 15,000 pounds of fresh fruit, which dries to approximately ten percent of the fresh weight. Guatemala had suffered a national disaster, so with the help of Mercy Ships, much of the product was transported and distributed by YWAM missionaries. The remainder was sent to the developing YWAM campus of the University of the Nations, in Kona, Hawaii.

It was a time of learning by trial and error and the learning curve was quite steep! In an early newsletter, Wally commented on the food value retained through the dehydration process. Here are his observations:

Food Value In Dehydrated Peaches

Very often, I am asked about the food value in dehydrated fruit. Below is a comparison between peaches canned in syrup versus dehydration, from the U.S. Department of Agriculture. (See Table on next page.)

Dehydrated Peaches

	gm Protein	mg Calcium	Total gm Carbs & Fiber	mg Vit. C	mg Iron
Canned in Syrup	1.8	18	91.2	13	1.4
Dehydrated	21.8	81	399.2	63	15.9

	mg Phosphate	I.U. Vit. A	mg Potassium	mg Ribr.	mg Niacin
Canned in Syrup	54	1,950	590	.11	2.5
Dehydrated	695	22,680	22,680	.43	35.2

During the off-season, the fall of 1981 to the spring of 1982, Wally researched the fruit processing industry and determined to acquire an automated "cutter" that would cut the peach in half and remove the pit. It was installed temporarily in the Yettem plant in time for the 1982 fruit season. Chuck Chamberlin, a YWAMer serving in Hawaii, spent countless hours during the hot summer months of 1982 and 1983 installing equipment to further mechanize the processing process. During the off-season between 1982 and 1983, the FMC Corporation of San Jose, California, donated two cutter machines and provided free servicing for over ten years! The addition of cutters enabled Gleanings to greatly increase their production. In 1983, using local volunteer workers, 106,000 pounds of fresh fruit was processed. Beginning that year and for the next six years, all dried product was shipped to Thailand to aid in the feeding program for the Cambodian refugees. Indeed, Wally had succeeded in providing the Gleanings of the San Joaquin Valley to the refugees who had so deeply touched him! If only he knew what great things lay ahead for this pioneer ministry, for from such humble beginnings, great things were yet to come!

CHAPTER 3
CUYAMA: A TRUE VEGGIE TALE

*For I know the plans I have for you, declares the Lord,
plans to prosper you and not to harm you, plans
to give you hope and a future.* Jeremiah 29.11

B y 1984, the Gleanings staff was increasing and needed a permanent home. Wally, ever the visionary, began to dream of being able to supplement the meager diet of the Cambodian refugees with nutritious vegetables as well as fruit. The possibility of dehydrating vegetables excited him! While attending trade shows, he learned of thousands of tons of cull carrots being thrown away or used as cattle feed. Could this be the beginning of a vegetable soup mix?

Many of the commercial carrot farms were located near Bakersfield, California, and the surrounding fertile valleys. As word of the Gleanings endeavor spread, businesman Bill Bolthouse, of Bolthouse Farms, in Cuyama, California, contacted Wally with an offer too good to refuse: the donation of a packing plant on two acres of land near the carrot fields! What an answer to prayer!

The town of Cuyama was originally built to accommodate the workers for a local oil company. The primary oil facility had closed and housing was very reasonable and immediately available. This became the California home of Wally and Norma, Joe and Betty Conway, Todd Stair, and other fellow YWAMers.

Together they labored to create a vision of feeding the hungry within the empty walls of a packing shed. They hung drywall, installed electrical wiring that would be sufficient to handle the future processing equipment. Renovations, new construction, landscaping, and equipment acquisition caused this season to be filled with hope and promise. The small but hard working staff, led by their energetic leader, put in long days and many hope-filled prayers to see their dream fulfilled.

As the fledgling ministry began, they trusted God for everything. Starting from scratch meant purchasing or praying for specific donations to meet their machinery and production needs. Forklifts, steam peelers, boilers, control panels, walkways, electrical units, and a host of other components would be required to make the "veggie plant" operational. In those early days Wally participated in industrial auctions prayerfully bidding on various components. Amazingly the items purchased, with minimal adjustments, always worked perfectly together!

Perhaps the greatest find was a natural gas dehydrator. It had a continuous belt nearly 200 feet long and would be able to produce 250,000 (4 oz.) servings of dehydrated carrots per twenty-four-hour period. Much excited conversation occurred as they calculated the numbers of hungry refugees who would gain much needed vitamins and nutrients through their efforts. The dehydrator was the crown jewel of the Cuyama veggie plant. Arriving on a large flat bed truck, it took all the staff, additional volunteers, several large forklifts, and a lot of ingenuity to maneuver it into position! With the final pieces of machinery in place, surely it would not be long before the production lines would be rolling in rich orange carrots.

The county of Santa Barbara where Cuyama was located was reputed as having the strictest environmental laws in the nation. At every turn, it seemed, the process of gaining full approval hit snags. First, the necessary permit process was lengthy and then there were revisions the county required to Wally's plans. A large pond was required for fire safety, a state of the art method of handling the waste water used in processing carrots was installed, and a myriad of other county mandates were met.

While Cuyama remained their home, in the spring of 1985 and 1986 they traveled to Yettem to hastily set up the fruit processing equipment. For ten to twelve weeks each summer, they would live with a divided focus, maintaining the ongoing work at Cuyama while continuing with the fruit dehydration in the Central Valley.

Realizing that the work load was greater than his staff could carry, Wally visited several YWAM locations in Oregon, California, Washington, and Canada recruiting for summer help during the fruit season. YWAM's Discipleship Training School (DTS) Program seemed an easy fit, particularly when two months of each five-month school was committed to an outreach project. When Wally shared with passion of the plight of the hungry refugees with the Canadian DTS, hardly a dry eye could be found! By 1984, the Salem, Oregon DTS had committed to participate for several weeks.

Among them Dave Romero and Candi (destined to be Candi Romero) were early Salem volunteers who in 1990, made a long-term commitment and significant contribution to Gleanings. In 1986 the Salem DTS was joined by the Richmond, BC, Canada DTS who spent three weeks at Yettem. Each team braved austere living conditions, sleeping on the floor and the pews of a small nearby church without air conditioning, garden hose showers for the guys, long work days in the extremely hot San Joaquin sun, and intensive hard labor with the fruit. With this young and energetic work force, the production increased annually from 106,000 lbs. of fresh fruit processed in 1982 to 240,000 in 1984 and over 500,000 in 1986!

At the end of each day, the volunteers would be blessed by another hearty meal miraculously prepared by Norma in the tiny kitchen of their travel trailer. There was always more than enough and regular delightful desserts of fresh local watermelon or tasty treats from Svenhardts Swedish bakery (a favorite with Wally!).

Throughout each long summer, everyone pulled together to accomplish the task at hand. Of all the helpers, no one portrayed servanthood more than Norma Wenge. Daily her home was invaded by DTS girls seeking a (brief!) shower; all the while, she provided meal after delicious meal. If Wally was the engine driving this project, then Norma was definitely its heart and soul.

By early September, the weary troops would journey back to their Cuyama homes and busy themselves with preparing the veggie plant. Although the Cuyama plant would never fulfill the big dreams Wally envisioned, still it became a catalyst for future development. Years later, using the analogy of a ship, Wally would comment that it was impossible to guide a docked ship; only one in motion could be turned, steered at the Captain's command. Gleanings was steaming ahead, and the Captain was fully in command. The Wenges and their staff were listening for God's directions. They celebrated each gain and grieved each setback. Setbacks meant hungry children, and that simply wasn't tolerable!

Ever a man of faith, Wally knew that more needed to be done. "Faith demonstrated by works" was the mandate, and the man found a new mission: raising the necessary funds for development and operation of the Yettem and Cuyama plants. Fixing his goal in clear view, he determined to find an active solution. Why not bike across America with the message of Gleanings? He would raise both awareness of the ministry and financial support! Anyone interested in joining?

CHAPTER 4
BIKES AND PLEDGES:
RACING TOWARD THE FUTURE

Brothers, I do not consider myself yet to have taken hold of it.
But one thing I do; forgetting what is behind and straining
toward what is ahead. I press on toward the goal to win the prize
for which God has called me heavenward in Christ Jesus.
Philippians 3.13–14.

I t was a routine visit to his family doctor, an annual
check-up required by Wally's life insurance
provider. The doctor, a family friend, shocked him
with these words: "Wally, you're only fifty-four. If you
want not only long life, but also quality of life, you need
more exercise!" Those comments challenged him, and
ever ready for a challenge, Wally determined to whip
himself into shape!

At fifty-four, jogging seemed out of the question, so
biking became the exercise of choice. He purchased
a racing bike and attacked his newly resolved fitness
regime with his customary passion. Hopping on his

new bike for its inaugural trip, he cycled determinedly out the driveway. His first goal was a five-mile loop. Returning minutes later, he dismounted and collapsed, struggling to catch his breath! Norma was terrified, concerned that he was having a heart attack, and that she would lose him!

Wally moderated his exercise and slowly built up to fifty to sixty miles per day. During inclement weather he would peddle for an hour or more, on a stationary bike, "to keep his legs." Eventually, the idea was birthed to marry his new activity with his ministry passion: feeding the hungry. He could bike across the country and raise funds for the work of Gleanings. (By this time, annual processing costs exceeded $20,000). Donors could sponsor Wally and his partners by the mile or with a fixed amount. Norma would follow, pulling their travel trailer along the route as a support vehicle and on road accommodations. The idea was birthed and Wally went about preparing to make it a reality.

After training in earnest, Wally and Rodkey Faust embarked on the first cross-America tour in 1983. They started in Santa Monica, California, and finished in Burkville, Virginia. The journey took thirty-seven days and covered 3,027 miles. Rodkey was a young YWAM missionary kid, holding the impressive distinction of being the youngest person to compete in Hawaii's Ironman Triathlon and a very fit Triathlete. He would regularly cycle 100 miles before work each day, and in him, Wally had a fitting partner. Through donations, nearly $15,000 was generated for the fruit processing and dehydration and the early development of the mission.

By 1985, Wally determined to utilize the same action plan by cycling 1,600 miles from Vancouver, BC, Canada, down the West Coast of the United States to Tijuana, Mexico. His September journey would be accompanied by two fellow cyclers: Eric Irwin, a YWAMer, and Bill Darrah, Jr, a friend of the mission. The Cuyama facility had recently been donated to Gleanings and there was much to do to make it operational. They were prepared physically and administratively for their endeavor. Pledge cards were delivered to family and friends, neighbors were contacted, and letters of recommendation were prepared. The following copy of the pledge card demonstrated for Eric the careful thoughtfulness that Wally placed on planning the Cuyama program: Each machine on his wish list was itemized, materials needed (i.e., concrete and fencing) were stated and the donors were given a clear overview of the purpose of the Bike-A-Thon.

Your Pledge Will Help Us Buy What Is Needed To Get Us Going!

Vegetable Dicer	$10,000 Donated
20 H.P. Submersible Pump, 13 stage	10,000
100 H.P. Boiler	20,000
Steam Peeler	25,000
Centrifuge	15,000 Donated
Product Moisture Tester	5,000
20' x 120' Metal Building	20,000
6 Foot Chainlink Fence	3,000
Cementing Critical Areas of the Yard	10,000
Truck Tractor, Diesel	15,000

Two 24' Flat Bed Trailers	5,000
Carrot Bins for Flat Bed Trailers	2,000 Donated
40' Trailer Van	10,000
Dump Truck	10,000
Pick-up Truck, Heavy Duty	10,000
3,000 lb Electric Forklift	5,000 Donated
6,000 lb Gas Forklift	8,000
200 Four Foot Vegetable Bins	8,000
Box Sealer Tape	2,500
Office, Shop, Rest Rooms, etc.	20,000
Office Equipment	2,000
Transporting Equipment	5,000
Overhauling Equipment	25,000
Installing Equipment, Incl. Electrical	30,000
Architect and County Planning Fees	5,000
Plant and Vehicle Insurance	6,000
	$ 254,500

California growers will *give* us all the fruit and vegetables we can transport and process for the hungry!

All pledges, gifts, and donations of equipment are tax deductible. Please, send in the tear-off response with your pledge today!

Gleanings for the Hungry Bike-A-Thon

Eric,

☐ I want to help feed the hungry by sponsoring this Bike-A-Thon.

Here is my pledge of ☐ 20¢ ☐ 10¢ ☐ 5¢ ☐ 1¢ ☐ Other _____ per mile
(e.g. 1600 x 5 ¢)

☐ My gift is enclosed.

☐ Here is my gift of $ _____ as a set amount to help get you going.

☐ Please keep me informed on the ministry of **GLEANINGS FOR THE HUNGRY.**

Name _____

Address _____

City _____ Zip _____

Mail To:

Gleanings for the Hungry
P.O. Box 34
Cuyama, CA 93214

Thank you for your generous gift.

Loren Cunningham, International Director for YWAM (now a respectable, twenty-three-year-old ministry), wrote an affirming letter of introduction and reference for the largely unknown ministry of YWAM called Gleanings for the Hungry.

I want to make you aware of a vital ministry that I'm sure you will want to be a part of.

Gleanings for the Hungry, an important arm of Youth With a Mission's Ministries, directed by my good friends and co-workers Wally and Norma Wenge, takes seriously Jesus' admonition in Matthew 25 to minister to the needs of the hungry.

For the past four years, Gleanings for the

Hungry has proven themselves to be effective in helping to relieve world hunger through their fruit dehydration plant outside Fresno, California. Their cost effective ability to secure and utilize fruit, discarded by growers as unusable in U.S. markets, and dehydrate it for distribution in needy areas of the world has benefited thousands of refugees in Guatemala and along the Thai/Cambodian border. They now have the ability to cut and dry one-half million pounds of fresh fruit each summer which will give a month's supply of fruit to 50,000 hungry people.

Gleanings for the Hungry has recently been given a large vegetable packing plant in Cuyama, California, which they plan to convert to a vegetable dehydration facility. When completed, the plant will be able to process 50,000 pounds of fresh carrots or potatoes each day for only pennies per pound. This amount will serve a daily vegetable portion to 200,000 needy people.

The Lord has put it on Wally's heart to bicycle from Vancouver, Canada, to Tijuana, Mexico, this September to raise money to complete this renovation project vital to helping the countless starving of our world. Your pledge of one, five, ten, or twenty cents per mile (or any fixed amount) over this 1,600-mile Gleanings for the Hungry Bike-A-Thon will literally go a long way toward making this critically needed facility to feed the hungry a reality

I urge you to pray and ask the Lord how you are to help this proven, practical, and effective ministry. Any gift or pledge will be a great encouragement to Wally as he bicycles these 1,600 miles for this tremendous cause. The new vegetable dehydration facility will help alleviate the suffering of thousands of hungry people world-wide.

I believe the Lord in this ministry, I believe in Wally, and I believe in you to do what you can to help.

May the Lord bless you.

Yours in Christ.

/signed/

Loren Cunningham

International Director

Youth With A Mission

Armed with a plan, his cycling comrades Eric and Bill, the letters of recommendation of Loren Cunningham, and the support of generous donors, Wally and friends departed Vancouver, BC, on September 1. The 1,600-mile journey to Tijuana was traversed in twenty-five days. They raised nearly $25,000 in gifts and pledges, to aid their ongoing work.

Ever a man of action, Wally pressed on with vigor

to see both the fruit plant in Yettem and the veggie plant quickly operational. He recruited staff, he visited YWAM schools to recruit, and he visited the offices of factories and canneries for equipment donations. An impassioned speaker, he regularly spoke in churches, at their request, to raise the awareness both of the plight of the needy and the ministry of Gleanings. Indeed his was a faith with works!

The work was becoming established; summer teams from YWAM, Discipleship Training Schools (DTS), and churches were supplying the necessary work force. Everything seemed to be falling into place nicely. This seemed to be a season of favor and fulfillment for all the staff. Then, the unimaginable occurred!

In April 1987, just nine weeks before the start of the summer fruit season, Wally received a call that was to reshape the ministry and refocus them for the future. The owner of the Yettem property who had so generously shared his facility with Gleanings for the previous five summers had fallen upon financial hardships. The bank was foreclosing and Wally had only days to remove his stored, fruit-processing machinery!

The question swirled his mind, where would they relocate? Surely, Cuyama was too far from their fruit suppliers for the lengthy transport to be practical. Would they even have a season in 1987? Yet, the refugees were still hungry and the YWAM missionaries responsible for distributing food depended on the Gleanings fruit as a dietary supplement. If the season was to be salvaged, where could they establish themselves on such short notice? Teams were scheduled, where would they stay? Would he have to cancel them?

A quick trip to a local realtor, Terrance Barnes, a friend of the ministry, seemed to confirm the impossibility of the situation. This prime agricultural valley was entering its busy season; there was nothing available on the market for purchase, rent, or lease. With a broken heart, Wally made plans to ship the fruit equipment to Cuyama for storage, while awaiting the Lord's new direction.

Calling Norma before leaving Yettem, he shared his inability to find a remedy to this sudden crisis; he would leave soon and would be home by the end of the day. While parking the car, he received an excited phone call from Terrance Barnes: a property had just come on the market!

Sensing God's guidance, they made immediate plans to view this former, tomato-packing facility on ten acres. It had a large, covered, packing area (perfect for the fruit-processing machinery), offices, cold storage, dining and coffee room for workers, and enough land for future development. Its location? Sultana, just two miles from Dinuba and the church, Wellspring Christian Center, which had been so instrumental in the early days of the ministry's development.

They prayed, sought godly counsel, and financial advice. Within days, they were able to arrange for necessary financing and take possession of the new facilities that would eventually become the heart of the ministry!

The clock was ticking, the summer was almost upon them, and Wally sprang into action. Always up for the challenge, he called in reinforcements! Friends, family, skilled tradesmen, and common laborers converged on the Sultana property with phenomenal results. In just nine weeks, the former tomato packing shed, was converted into a fruit processing plant. Machinery was installed, the first sulfur house was built, shower and dormitory facilities were provided, and a small outdoor kitchen area was established. Although hastily created, it was adequate for the summer teams, would allow the fruit dehydration to continue, and best of all: it was their own!

Each visiting team would view slides taken in places like Cambodia, Thailand, or the Philippines, emphasizing the desperate need for nutritious food. Wally would then share inspirationally of the part we could play in rescuing the needy and demonstrating, very practically, God's loving heart. The session would conclude with the faith inspiring story of God's guidance in establishing this faith mission! Tears were shed, and team members would attack the week's back-breaking work with a sense of passion and purpose!

Although the fruit season was shortened in 1987, with a June 27 delayed start, the salvaged fruit year yielded an estimated 40,000 pounds of dried peaches and nectarines. In the July 1987 Gleanings newsletter, Wally states that the dried product would be sent to aid the "Cambodian refugee children, nursing mothers, and pregnant women." His prayer request was: "That those receiving our fruit will understand that there is a loving Heavenly Father who cares enough about them to lay it on our hearts and yours to provide the fruit for them." The vision was simple and extraordinarily focused: feed the hungry and demonstrate God's love.

The terms of purchase for the Sultana property allowed a deferred deposit of $30,000 due in October 1987, with the full $130,000 due as a balloon payment by the fall of 1989. Here is how Wally described it in a Gleanings Newsletter:

> The terms of purchase called for $30,000 at the date of escrow, $30,000 in July of 1988, and $70,000 in June of 1989. John Kalendar had trouble with the surveillance report and finally got everyone together to get it cleared up. The escrow was closed in June of 1988. By this time, I had one-half of the $30,000 and had to borrow the balance from the YWAM fund. In July of 1988, I again only had $15,000 and had to borrow another $15,000. That fall, the International Council met in Cimaron, Colorado. I told Loren I had to raise $100,000 in the next two months. He prayed for me. I prayed for two weeks telling the Lord that I knew I had to do something, but I wanted to do it His way. The Lord spoke to me, "Wally, you have not because you ask not." I realized I had to telephone people. We saw the $94,000 come in and the party I owed $6,000 called

to say, "Pay me later." We made the $70,000 payment on time. The Lord did it."

Consequently, before the equipment was set up and running, Wally was training for his third and final bike trip. Early each morning, he would cycle sixty miles, shower, have breakfast, and greet the team at 8:00 a.m. to start the day's fruit processing. His inspiring work ethic earned him the admiration of every summer team member!

By midsummer, over $7,000 was pledged toward this Bike-A-Thon. With Norma and three others driving a car and towing their sixteen foot travel trailer, Wally and Tom began the arduous 2,307-mile trip. Departing from Portland, Maine, on August 19, they pedaled toward their destination: Key West, Florida. Like on the previous two occasions, all went well until Friday September 11.

Distracted by a passing car, Wally and his biking partner collided, and Wally tumbled to the ground at full speed. Having his feet strapped into the bike stirrups made it impossible to break his fall and he suffered a severe fractured femur. Surgery followed, and a long stainless steel pin was inserted to provide stability while the bone mended. His biking partner finished the last one and a half days alone while Wally rested uncomfortably in the Palm Beach Gardens Medical Center.

Wally convalesced in the hospital until the morning of August 21, when the doctor released him. The team helped Wally into the car and they started driving for home at 9:30 am! According to Wally's journal:

"I did okay in the back seat today and we drove about 372 miles – thank you, Lord Jesus!"

Down but not out, he hobbled around Gleanings, overseeing the off-season development of the Sultana property. His leg in a cast, supported by crutches, Wally recognized that his Heavenly Father was establishing His ministry at Gleanings. The vision had been cast and with God as their strong supporter, they faced a bright future!

CHAPTER 5
DEDICATION DAY: JUNE 11, 1989

*I will praise you O Lord, among the nations; I will sing
of you among the peoples. For great is your love, higher
than the heavens; your faithfulness reaches to the skies.
Be exalted, O God above the heavens, and let your
glory be over all the earth.* Psalm 108.3–5

Throughout 1988, the Sultana facility was shaped and forged into a full-time ministry location. Additional staff was added and daily the progress was noticeable. The good news about Gleanings was becoming better known and financial contributions increased considerably during this season. The favor of the Lord was on this project and the staff moved ahead at full steam!

In late fall 1988, Wally learned that the YWAM DTS from Fort St. John, BC, Canada, who had served as summer volunteers for three years, had lost their facility lease. Quickly, he shifted into action, seeing this as an opportunity to advance to another stage in Gleanings development. Wally invited Steve and Becky Witmer and their DTS staff to relocate their school to Sultana. The additional manpower would aid in the ongoing construction projects that were providing additional accommodation needed for the summer teams. He stated in the January 1989 newsletter:

> We want to utilize our fruit facility in the off season by making it available to other YWAM bases to run various mission training schools. Our British Columbia DTS has lost their lease and will run their school in Sultana beginning April 17. Without losing focus he continues by adding, "Simply, having adequate housing will allow us to accommodate more people so we can produce more dried fruit to help more people. Our production goal in 1989 is to process two million pounds of (fresh) fruit."

The British Columbia DTS joined Wally in his mission to expand the base. Arriving in January 1989, the DTS staff joined the Gleanings staff to accomplish yet another gigantic challenge: to convert a fruit processing plant into a DTS facility! Dorms were readied, bunk beds built, an eight-room "motel" started, the kitchen was renovated, and a dining room created.

April arrived and so did the DTS students. They studied in the mornings, being taught by a wonderful cast of visiting YWAM speakers. Several hours a day the DTS students and staff would work to ready the plant for the summer fruit season and another project: the dedication of this new facility.

The date was set: June 11, 1989. Guests were invited and Loren Cunningham, YWAM founder and President, was requested to emcee the dedication service. Everyone at Gleanings pitched in to ready the facility for this celebration. A large cold storage room was emptied and painted. A large mural was designed and painted on the front wall along with this scripture from Matthew 25.35, 37, 40.

> ..."For I was hungry and you gave me something to eat...," ..."Lord when did we see you hungry and feed you...," The King will reply, "I tell you the truth, whatever you did for one of the least of these brothers of mine, you did for me."

This passage provided a visual back drop and a constant reminder, throughout the celebration, of the significant role Gleanings had to play in fulfilling the Lord's mercy directive.

The day dawned bright and the guests streamed into the sparkling property. Over 400 people from several states took seats in the cold storage unit turned auditorium. Special music, worship, inspiring sharing, and the history of Gleanings was presented. Wally captured everyone's interest by thanking the various growers who had donated fruit over the years and, through a multimedia presentation, showed the need of the recipients and the tonnage of dried fruit shipped.

A mountain of food was prepared and served! Roast beef, rice pilaf, salad, rolls and delicious cake for dessert.

Lesta Kelly, her crew from Wellspring Christian Center, and the Gleanings staff served the hungry guests.

Following the delicious lunch, 2,000 pounds of nectarines were processed through the machinery so everyone could see the equipment at work. Like a proud parent, Wally acted as tour guide, explaining the process. This was a day long awaited! The vision was being fulfilled and a dream had become a reality. The humble journey that began in 1981 by the will of God and a faith-filled servant, had now arrived at a debt-free facility, with operating equipment, dedicated staff, and many hungry people fed by the year 1989. Perhaps the best testimonial is found at the entrance of the facility. It says:

> *Not to us, oh Lord, not to us, but to your name be the glory....* Psalm 115.1.

CHAPTER 6
TOUCHING THE WORLD
WITH THE FRUIT OF GLEANINGS

Be imitators of God, therefore, as dearly loved children, and live
a life of love just as Christ loved us and gave Himself up for us
as a fragrant offering to God. Ephesians 5.1–2

Over the next decade, continued improvements of the processing machinery and additional staff and volunteers, enabled the production to increase dramatically. In 1989, the year of the dedication of the Sultana property, over two million pounds of fresh fruit were processed. Records for the year indicated that four forty-foot containers were shipped to Manila, Philippines, to aid the thousands living on the city's garbage dump. One forty-foot container was sent to Hong Kong for the Vietnamese boat people; a truckload was sent to Baja, Mexico, for the very poor Oaxacan Indians, and 10,000 pounds were sent to an

American Indian mission in Arizona. It was an exciting year, one filled with promise for greater ability to care for the needy.

Annually, production records were set and broken. What had taken the entire 1981 season to process was now accomplished in a single day! In 1991, the tenth anniversary of Gleanings, over two million pounds of fruit were processed. With increased supply came additional partners from various parts of the globe. YWAM's Mercy Ships transported and delivered fruit to the victims of Guatemala's earthquakes; YWAM Brazil provided fruit to remote Amazon tribes; the 700 Club paid for the trucking and ocean shipping of dried peaches to the residents of the Manila garbage dump; and private donors aided with trucking costs.

There are many amazing stories of the actual distribution methods of the Gleanings food. Sea going containers are the primary means for transoceanic shipping, but what happens when the products reach their destination? Trucks of every make and vintage make deliveries where road conditions allow, but often more creative and simple arrangements must be employed. River boats transported Gleanings food up the swollen Amazon and Mississippi Rivers; ox carts and even wheelbarrows were pressed into service to aid distribution in rural Africa and Asia. United Nations helicopters airlifted food to remote refugee camps, and youth smuggled food in their backpacks into restricted access areas. With each delivery, regardless of the methods, the love of God was tangibly communicated!

Perhaps one of the most inspiring stories of food distribution is that of a shipment to frigid Siberia in 1999. Gleanings became aware of the critical need of those living in a remote area of Siberia where many were in imminent danger of starvation. In partnership with the ministry of Samaritans Purse, 20,000 pounds of fruit was especially packed to fit into the cargo holds of aircraft. Alaska Airlines shipped the fruit, free of charge, to Nome, Alaska, on the Western shore of the state of Alaska. From here, Samaritans Purse flew the fruit to Sikuin, and utilizing large Russian military snowmobiles, the fruit was distributed to those who so desperately needed it.

There are many miraculous and amazing stories documenting the distribution of Gleanings food. The creativity exhibited can only be attributed to the creative genius of our loving God; for we see His hand guiding and intervening. He is our primary partner and demonstrates His involvement in myriads of ways!

In 1988, Wally and Norma had journeyed to Colonia Guerro in Baja Norte, Mexico, to visit the outreach location of the BC DTS. Touched by the difficult living conditions of the Oaxacan Indians, who largely subsisted as migrant field workers, they determined to make a difference. Partnering with Chuck and Charla Pereau, founders and directors of "Foundation for His Ministry," they began to ship fruit annually to help in their large orphanage and migrant labor camp outreaches. This letter from Charla dated May 1992, so beautifully communicates the impact Gleanings was having:

Dear Wally and all those wonderful friends who participated in the processing of Gleanings for the Hungry,

We're overwhelmed by your generous contribution of thousands of pounds of fruit for distribution to the destitute Oaxacan Indians that surround the Mission at Vincente Guerrero.

In this desert region of the Baja Peninsula, fruit is scarce, of poor quality, and exorbitantly expensive. For the poor, it is an unaffordable luxury; yet, we all know that fruit is essential to our well-being. Hundreds of little children's faces are covered with blotches of pigment discoloration because of malnutrition. Our clinic provides ointment to be applied to these dry patches, but because of your kindness, we can treat the cause.

I wish each of those who helped in the processing could personally receive the thanks and the hugs from His little ones in Mexico.

A significant shift occurred in the summer of 1991. Wally was approached by a neighbor who was preparing to sell 11.6 acres of land adjacent to the Gleanings property. Was he interested? Absolutely! With fresh vision, he plunged into raising the $81,200, plus taxes, to purchase this parcel of land. Although covered with mature orange trees, this immediately provided a solution that would simplify the ministry: This acreage would house the veggie plant!

The consolidation of both the fruit and veggie dehydration onto one property would make it possible to focus on both aspects of the Gleanings ministry at the same time and provide additional stability for the staff. The Sultana property would be spacious enough to provide permanent housing for staff, adequate accommodation for summer teams and mission's builders, and office space for the ministry. One additional benefit was that Tulare County was friendly to agri-businesses and had looked favorably on the development of the existing Gleanings property.

Here is how Wally described this event in His diary:

> John said, "Wally, I need $7,000 per acre." I told him we could be serious about that, but that I did not have any money. I told him I would have to raise it. He wanted to know how long that would take and I told him ninety days. He said okay. We had the papers prepared in escrow and John contacted a surveyor. When the surveyor was done, it turned out to be 11.6 acres, for a total price of $81,200.

> It was the wrong time of the year to buy the property. We had no money, not even the money to get sulfur for the fruit so we could start the process line, and there was the big cost of food, etc.

> As the summer went on, we paid every bill on time and had the $81,200 one week early. All praise goes to the Lord for His wonderful provision.

Through gifts, pledges from friends of the ministry, and a matching grant of $25,000 from a generous foundation, Wally raised the funds, within the ninety-day escrow period! Again, God's hand of blessing was obvious. The debt-free ministry had just more than doubled both in size and in vision.

The next few years included a collision of very busy three-month-summer-fruit seasons and nine months of property development. There was always a new project or two (or twenty-two!) demanding the staff's attention. One memory stands out vividly for all of the workers during these years: It was the white board, filled with the "to-do-list" for the team. It was always numbered and listed in an orderly fashion, before Wally would leave for a recruiting trip. Diligently the team would stroke off one completed task after another, only to discover, upon Wally's return, that the list had been freshly replenished!

Indeed, this season was one of significant new development. Everywhere you looked, a metamorphosis was occurring! Some of the key projects completed during this period included:

◆ "8 complex" motel units completed
◆ Shower and Laundromat
◆ Woodshop
◆ Multi-purpose room built
◆ Many new machines installed for fruit processing
◆ Sulfur tunnels added
◆ New shop building donated
◆ Veggie plant assembled

- New septic system installed
- Beautiful staff housing acquired
- Landscaping around homes and plant
- Fire safety pond and hydrants installed
- New RV site for mission builders
- Concrete and more concrete!

A ministry city was arising out of the orchards of the San Joaquin valley: a place dedicated to God's purposes, fulfilling God's plan, and fully focused on their mission.

A task this extensive could not be accomplished without an army of willing workers. Many servant-hearted volunteers, both staff and mission's builders, graced Gleanings. Although the list is extensive, and represents many states and countries, a few come to mind from those initial days:

- Gordon and Lori Aldinger
- Joe and Betty Avilla
- Joe and Betty Conway
- Kobus and Patty Harmse
- Eliot and Connie Henderson
- Ralph and Linda Konkol
- Marge Masitti
- Len and Lois Nylin
- Jack and Carly Patten
- Steve and Joan Perkins and Family
- Betty and Hill Rasmussen
- Dave and Candi Romero
- Joel Skalinder
- Todd Stair

- Gil and Alice Vierra
- Steve and Becky Witmer
- Barry and Lori Witmer
- Dan Wine
- Agnes and Nathaniel Wolfe

The contribution made by these and so many nameless others is incalculable; their rewards are stored up securely in heaven!

The purpose of facility development was never simply to provide better equipment or accommodations. In the end it was about alleviating hunger. Each successive fruit season saw greater capacity and enhanced production. More fruit, more people fed, more ministries aided in more countries. The impact and scope of Gleanings was expanding.

In 1997 and 1998, Wally again opened the facility, during the off-season, for a YWAM Crossroads Discipleship Training School. Willie and Diane Williams, who had been so instrumental at the beginning of Gleanings, were returning after thirteen years of serving with YWAM overseas.

Having served as staff and leaders of many Crossroads DTS schools for married couples and adults, their expertise, coupled with their heart for Gleanings, made them a perfect fit. They dove into the life of the Gleanings, contributing their enthusiasm and passion for the poor to the base. The September 1997 Crossroads DTS had twelve students and in January 1998, the students went to serve in Mexico as part of their outreach. While there, they focused on construction projects at a Bible School in Valle de Las Palmas, including the construction of a water storage tank for future agricultural projects.

The team served local orphanages by preparing nutritious meals, leading worship and evangelism meetings, playing with the children and providing an abundance of loving hugs. Additionally, they traveled into mountainous regions, delivering food, clothes, and medicine to a Paipai Indian village.

September 1998 saw the next Crossroads DTS with a total of eighteen wonderful students. Their outreach, in January and February 1999, led them to Nicaragua where they demonstrated the love of God in practical ways, to the displaced victims of a volcanic eruption. These precious people had lost everything in this traumatic natural disaster. Upon arrival, they discovered ninety desperate survivors huddling under a ten-by-ten-foot tin awning. In co-operation with YWAM's Mercy Ship, they were able to assist in the rebuilding of homes and the establishing of small business ventures.

Indeed, Gleanings was maturing and becoming a launching pad for ministry to "the least of these, my brothers."

CHAPTER 7
MATURING OF THE MINISTRY

...being confident of this, that He who began a good work in you, will carry it on to completion until the day of Christ Jesus. Philippians 1.6

The 1991 acquisition of 11.6 acres of adjoining land enabled the Gleanings ministry to not only expand food production but also provide the opportunity to have improved housing for the hard-working staff. These selfless servants focused on the purpose of providing for the poor, rather than their own personal comforts.

Leading by example, as they always did, Wally, Norma, and her sister lived for ten months in a tiny sixteen-foot travel trailer. Wally often chuckled that the measurements were from tongue to rear bumper, because the trailer only measured twelve feet long inside! From this cramped and cozy situation, Norma also cooked for the summer fruit teams and volunteers who came to serve in the off-season. Using her two-burner stove, she uncomplainingly served up the heartiest and most delicious meals for the weary workers.

Finally, at the insistence of staffer Gil Vierra, Wally conceded and started the remodel of the former packing shed office into a tiny two room apartment for Norma and himself. Just in time for the 1988 fruit season, they took occupancy and enjoyed this compact privacy for the next seven years.

Additionally, all the Gleanings staff was living in very tight quarters. Dave and Candi Romero were living with their three children in a one room apartment. Dave and Candi had served YWAM for fourteen years in Salem, Oregon, Jamaica, and Gleanings for the Hungry. Dave provided oversight for the summer teams, while Candi gave leadership to the kitchen.

Elliot and Connie Henderson and their two young children also shared a single room in the "eight-plex motel." Elliot and Connie met while working with YWAM in the Philippines for four and one half years. Joining the Gleanings' staff in 1990, they added their skills and energy to the growing ministry. Two manufactured homes were purchased in 1995 and provided spacious and welcomed accommodation for these hard-working staff.

By 1998, it was apparent that additional staff housing was needed. The following is an excerpt from Wally's journal.

In January of 1998, I put out a newsletter asking for help to buy another double-wide mobile home and I did the same thing in February. Our total for the two months was only $8,000 towards a mobile home and yet we needed about $75,000. We continued to pray for that. In the meantime, I wrote to two different foundations asking them to pray about giving us a helping hand. The one in Colorado was not in a position to do anything at that time. The one from SG Foundation sent a man over by the name of John, who spent four and one half hours with us and gave a report to the foundation. In turn, they gave us $50,000 toward the mobile home! Now we're down to needing $15,000 more. We had two people who came by and between the two of them, they gave $5,000. Now we only needed $10,000 to pay cash for it.

The Howard Ahmanson Foundation from Southern California had promised two years before to send some money, and yet I did not know how they were going to designate it or what they were going to do. It came in as a general designation, so we were able to take $10,000 out of that and we paid cash for the mobile home. Another of God's great provisions.

The 1990s were years of rapid development. Each year during the winter and spring, the facility would experience renovation and improvement. New fruit processing equipment made it possible to produce large quantities of dried peaches and nectarines. Larger volumes necessitated larger teams of summer volunteers to assist with this endeavor.

And come they did! By the late 1990s, teams of seventy-five were required to work weekly during early June to mid-September. Housing and feeding this army of volunteer workers created extraordinary challenges. Using his excellent planning and design skills, Wally (and staff) built dormitories, kitchen and dining hall, laundry and shower blocks, and a multi-purpose recreation area for the youth.

Summer days were busy times for staff and volunteers. The hot, dry Sultana days were perfect for the rapid dehydration of the ripe peaches and nectarines. Everyone worked hard and the rewards were daily calculated in statistics like:

◆ Number of bins of fresh fruit processed
◆ Number of buckets of dry fruit packaged
◆ Estimate of servings of dried fruit provided, and a host of similar discussions.

These indicators became the motivation to try harder and shatter yesterday's records for the sake of the poor!

The Bethesda Foundation, a benevolent group, had generously contributed to the Gleanings endeavor for several years. During the summer of 1996, Bethesda Foundation Directors visited Gleanings for the Hungry to see the fruit plant in operation. They were amazed by the volumes of fruit being produced and the diligence of the volunteer teams. While watching the youth, they recognized one area that could dramatically improve the experience for the young workers - a swimming pool! The aptly named "Pool of Bethesda" was made possible by their generous grant and is without question the after work highlight for every summer team.

During 1997 and 1998, the Gleanings team, augmented by an army of volunteers, began the assembly of the new vegetable processing plant. This development would enable the ministry to launch into new varieties of dehydrated food products, and extend the season beyond the intense and condensed summer season. Ever the bargain hunter, Wally had located a large steel building, which was formally used as an olive-packing shed. Purchasing this at an auction, they disassembled and moved the entire building to the Sultana site. Over the next eighteen months, Wally's dream became a reality: Gleanings could provide dehydrated, nutritious vegetables to supplement the diet of the world's hungry. The critical plan was to process carrots from the San Joaquin Valley and dry them using a "continuous belt dryer," which would be located in the new vegetable plant. Wally estimated that this dryer could run twenty-four hours, fifty-two weeks per year, and provide 250,000 four-ounce servings per day. Unfortunately, Wally did not see the fulfillment of his dream. The vegetable plant would provide many nutritious products, but only after he was received into the Father's glory.

CHAPTER 8
OH, HOW THE MIGHTY HAVE FALLEN

Your glory, O Israel, lies slain on your heights.
How the mighty have fallen! 2 Samuel 1.19

Wally Wenge was a man renowned for his compassion, boundless energy, and focused passion for the mission God had entrusted to him. The possibility of slowing down never entered his mind; there was simply too much to do!

What a shock it was when Wally announced his illness in the November 1998 newsletter. Using the "Bad News – Good News" format, he expressed the situation clearly:

BAD NEWS – and now it's my turn:

In the spring of 1996, I first noticed that I was short of breath when doing hard work. I just thought I was out of shape and needed to do more exercise. In March 1997 while Norma and I were in South Africa for meetings, I realized in walking hills that I ran out of breath very quickly, and that something was wrong. After many tests, my pulmonary Doctor told us in May of 1997 that I had a severe case of Idiopathic Pulmonary Fibrosis. The doctors don't know how I got this and there is no medical cure. Our medical journal says that when you are severe you have no more than one year to live — So according to that, my funeral should have been last May.

GOOD NEWS

I am a living miracle. My volume of air in the fall of 1997 was 3.4 or forty-five percent of normal. In October 1998, I had another test for my lung volume and it is still 3.4 percent. Since this is a very progressive disease, this is a miracle! Further, last year I was out of breath walking across the street and up the five steps of my house. Today, I can walk fast, up to forty or fifty steps, before being out of breath.

God does not promise to shield you and me from all problems, but he does promise to go with us through the problems. This Thanksgiving and throughout the year, let us give our Lord the praise and thanks for His faithfulness in being with us through all the problems and hardships.

Although his illness was incurable, he remained upbeat and faithful to God's calling. His thanksgiving to God filled that November newsletter and challenged all his supporters to "...give our Lord the praise for His faithfulness in being with us through all the problems and hardships." Faithful and God-focused, Wally was an amazing man.

Neither magnificent trees nor mighty men are created in a day. The process of the shaping of the man, Wally Wenge, into the mighty man of God, required a lifetime of sacrifice, obedience, and dedication in the face of overwhelming odds. The following is a brief sampling of the pathway that Wally and Norma journeyed. Perhaps their story will be an inspiration for all of us who follow.

Wally was raised by a godly Swedish mother and a Norwegian father, who taught him to love and obey the commands of the Lord. By the time he was seventeen, the Second World War was raging. Released from an apprentice electrical program, he joined the Merchant Marines, earning a number of certificates.

Wally and Norma had been teenage sweethearts and upon the completion of the war, they were married. Here is how Wally comically records the story leading up to their marriage:

> We wanted to get married when I was nineteen and she was eighteen, but my folks said, "No, you need to be of age, twenty-one." It was Grandma Hansen who was pretty practical. She said, "Oh, you should let the kids get

married. They're staying up all hours of the night ruining their health. Besides, its more fun when you're younger." So mom finally said, "Okay, twenty years of age." So on August 22, I was twenty, and we got married on August 24, 1947. And that's the reason why my birthday and our anniversary are so close together. We weren't going to wait any longer. On our honeymoon, we went back to Minnesota where I introduced Norma to all the relatives.

When Norma and I got our marriage license in Salinas, dad had to go in and sign for it. I had a movie camera at that time and mom was outside taking pictures as we came out. However, when Norma and I came out, dad didn't come. He had stayed back because he knew it was our moment. He was very sensitive to that fact. Then, a few minutes later, he walked out on his own.

In 1999, Wally gives this moving testimonial:

To my recollection, I believe I have told Norma that I loved her every day we've lived together. We've had an incredible marriage. I still love her now, more than ever.

After his tour of duty with the Merchant Marines, Wally entered civilian life, working in a variety of jobs as an electrician and refrigeration expert for five years. Eventually he settled into a career with Sears, his starting wage was $1.50 per hour! By 1957, he was promoted to service manager for the Salinas Sears Store. Eighteen months later, he was again promoted to service manager for the Northern California region. Rapidly he climbed the ladder of success within Sears, serving various stores in the roles of Assistant Manager and Superintendent. His remarkable leadership skills had opened many doors and employment opportunities, but this would soon become the source of a great test of faith.

By early 1971, Wally had connected with Loren Cunningham, the founder of YWAM, and God began to stir his heart for new things. Wally recorded these thoughts:

> In September of 1971, the Lord asked me a question: "Was Sears first in my life or was He first?" The answer was simple. The Lord was (and still is) first. However with the question came the understanding that if I said, "the Lord," He may ask me to quit Sears that day. After twenty-three years with a company you don't do something foolish. I weighed the question for three days. The gentle hand of the Lord was on me, not heavy, but it didn't go away. Finally, on the way to work I told the Lord He was first in my life and if He wanted me to quit, I would do it right away. When I said that, the Lord's hand lifted and I knew it was a test. Whee!
>
> In the fall of 1971 and spring of 1972, Norma and I knew the Lord was getting ready to do something new in our lives, but we didn't know what.

Taking a leave of absence from Sears, Wally and Norma traveled to Munich, Germany, to organize the massive YWAM Olympic Outreach. More than 1,000 people participated in this endeavor. Wally's Sears training paid off, since his last store had over 1,000 employees! By the end of August 1972, the Olympic Outreach had ended and the Wenges had a new directive – they were to quit Sears and join YWAM full-time! January 31 was Wally's last day at Sears, and on February 2, 1973, the Wenge family was on board a flight for Lausanne, Switzerland, and the beginning of many faithful years of YWAM service. A huge test of faith and obedience had been passed with flying colors and the Wenges were airborne.

The Wenges demonstrated admirable love and compassion for others. Wally and Norma had two biological children, Coleen and Steve. While Norma was pregnant with Steve, the rheumatic fever she contracted as a teen flared up. They were advised against additional pregnancies, being told that it would certainly cost Norma her life. With room in their hearts and home for more children, they applied to the Holt Adoption Agency in Georgia. Soon little Luanne was assigned to their care; they made the trip from California to Portland, Oregon, to happily receive their third child.

Applying again, they were granted another child whom they called Dwight. Traveling to Seattle, they gathered this new bundle of joy into their arms and began the trip home. This desire to lovingly embrace children demonstrates their compassionate hearts;

everyone was always welcomed in the Wenge home and into their circle of friends. Indeed this was a wonderful trait, since they would soon be called upon to care for the thousands of abandoned and orphaned children through the ministry of Gleanings for the Hungry.

Perhaps most telling of the character of the man, Wally Wenge, was the tender way he cared for Norma following a severe rear-end car accident in 1968. Here is a spartan summary of his extraordinary care, taken from the November 1998 Gleanings Newsletter:

> We have much to be thankful for — Yet, I know from the prayer requests that we receive that many of you are suffering with pain, grief, and hardships. I want to encourage you in the faithfulness of the Lord by a couple of pages from my life.
>
> In 1968, we were hit by a car going fifty-five miles an hour while we were stopped in a line of traffic. Norma received a severe whiplash that resulted in five neck fusions over twelve years. During this time, she spent almost all the time in bed because of the pain. The only way I could keep her out of the hospital was to start giving her pain shots; and before it was over, I had given her 12,000 pain shots and 3,000 shots for nausea. While this was not easy to go through, God's grace was so with us that it was like I lived above it. In the natural, this cannot be explained or understood, but it was a reality for me. Norma has been pain free since 1980 — God is good!

Over those twelve years, he patiently cared for Norma, administering 15,000 shots for pain and nausea. Eight of these pain-filled years were spent traveling with YWAM! Ultimately, in 1980 the final neck vertebrae operation was successful and Norma was able to return to a normal life—just before the start of Gleanings for the Hungry in 1982!

Never a complainer, Wally gently nursed Norma throughout those difficult years. He had lived with suffering, he had attempted to alleviate it in his family, and now God opened the doors for his faithful love to literally reach around the globe.

Wally was an extraordinary man, walking away from the pinnacle of his career, from the stability of a supervisor's income, to join YWAM, a faith mission. God was indeed number one in his life. He opened his heart and home to orphans, and continued to be an advocate for the widow and orphans. He lovingly cared for his wife, and modeled faithful love to all who knew him. This was the test of character, the strength of conviction, that enabled him to persevere through the difficult and stretching early days of Gleanings. He had learned well, passing his spiritual exams; now he was being promoted once again.

Idiopathic Pulmonary Fibrosis, that was the expert diagnosis. It was both incurable and considered fast growing. There was nothing anyone could do but trust and pray. It is unlikely that anyone could have guessed that just three short months after he revealed his condition in the ministry newsletter, Wally Wenge would make his final journey into the arms of Jesus.

Wally and Norma spent Christmas 1998 with friends in Bakersfield, CA. Two days later, his condition deteriorating quickly, he was driven to St. Agnes Hospital in Fresno. After eighteen days of hospital care, Wally was sent home, to his family and beloved Gleanings. Eight days later, January 22, 1999, surrounded by loving family, Wally passed away and walked lovingly into the Savior's embrace.

Although medical science did not conclusively prove the source of Wally's Pulmonary Fibrosis, the respiratory experts detected microscopic asbestos particles in his lungs. Because Wally never worked in areas where he would have been exposed to asbestos, the only reasonable answer is that his dedication to distance biking may have provided this exposure. Vehicles passing a cyclist tend to brake, slowing to safely pass. Older style automotive brakes contained asbestos fibers and braking releases microscopic particles into the air. Could it be that Wally's love for the ministry and his passion to do whatever it took to ensure that Gleanings succeeded, including biking fundraisers, could ultimately lead to his passing? If so, this would be another evidence of his love and commitment.

The Memorial Service was Tuesday, January 26, and was attended by over 400 friends and family. Several YWAM leaders, including Don Stephens and Leland Paris, participated, while Loren Cunningham spoke via satellite to those gathered. Pastor Doug Hagey presided, and Norma Wenge concluded that, "It was a beautiful

and honoring service, first to Jesus and then to Wally."
In her journal entry for that day, she penned:

> Wally would be missed; indeed he was a man
> of irreplaceable significance and spiritual
> stature. His passion and compassion raised
> the bar for those leaders who would follow in
> his footsteps.

As we close this chapter, a sensitive selection from
Norma's journal will provide a rare and intimate view
of their loving relationship.

> Friday, January 22, 1999.
>
> I don't know what to say. Today was Wally's
> home going. At 9:00 a.m., he silently slipped
> from this earth to meet Jesus in heaven. Oh,
> how I'd love to peek and see all that's going
> on—so many loved ones to greet him; I am
> jealous and very lonely already. Lord, I need
> you more than ever. Thank you for your
> grace, love, and support. Thank you, Lord,
> for forgiveness, love, mercy, and especially
> for a precious man of God for fifty-one and a
> half years.
>
> Saturday, January 23, 1999
>
> It will be days on end without you, my darling;
> I miss you so much. I am counting on you
> being there to greet me when I come. He was
> loved by so many. It's still so hard to believe
> my darling is really gone and will never come
> home again. Dear Lord, thank you for giving

me such a special relationship with such a special man...Lord, you promised to be the husband to the widow, be my comfort and peace I pray.

In the words of the Psalmist David, *Oh how the mighty have fallen.*

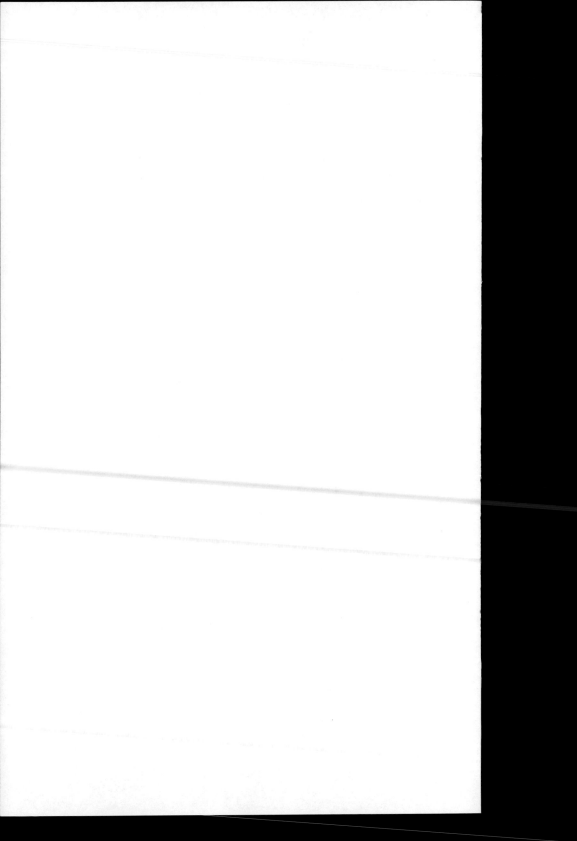

CHAPTER 9
FROM DEATH, NEW LIFE

I tell you the truth, unless a kernel of wheat falls into the ground
and dies, it remains only a single seed. But if it dies,
it produces many seeds. John 12.24

Wally's passing could have signaled the end of Gleanings for the Hungry, but that was not God's plan and purpose. The vision of Gleanings had been clearly communicated and planted deeply in the hearts of the committed staff. Wally had met personally with many of his dedicated staff, and true to character, had given each of them tasks to be accomplished in the advent of his passing. Indeed, the seed of faith had germinated and everyone pledged to move forward in ministry; furthering the cause of feeding the hungry.

On the eve of Wally Wenge's memorial service,

the Gleanings Board of Directors gathered (they had attended the memorial) to discuss the future of the mission. It was decided that one of their members, Len Nylin, would step into the interim leadership role for a six-month period. Len was well-known to the staff; regularly he served at Gleanings and would fill in occasionally when Wally attended YWAM leadership meetings. It is reported that when the announcement was made of Len Nylin's appointment, the staff stood and applauded!

There could not have been a better choice than Len. He was a childhood friend of Wally, having first met when they were ten years of age. As adults, they remained close and often connected as families spending time together. When Wally began the fledging Gleanings ministry, Len was one of the first to support his decision financially. Serving on the Gleanings Board for many years provided him with an intimate view of the ministry's strengths and future development plans. Little did he know that his six-month term of Interim Director would become five and one half years!

In the March 1999 newsletter, Len Nylin introduces himself to the Gleanings financial partners. Here is what he said:

> Please, let me introduce myself. My name is Lennard Nylin. As I write this letter, I realize Wally has been gone for only a few days. Wally and I grew up together, he was my dear friend, and we all miss him immensely. I have served for the past ten years as one of the board of

directors for Gleanings for the Hungry. In the past, I have filled in during Wally's absence from the base for prolonged trips. I always enjoyed the opportunity and excitement of all that was accomplished at Gleanings. I am retired as director of Manufacturing and Development and director of Research and Development in a corporation for twenty years. The board met following Wally's death and voted to place the responsibility of directorship upon my shoulders. I have willingly accepted and the staff has warmly received me and responded to my leadership. My wife Lois has agreed to serve beside me, and together we committed to do our very best to lead Gleanings forward. Please let me assure you that the vision God gave Wally for Gleanings for the Hungry is shared by all of us on the board, and the missionaries serving on the base in Sultana. We will accept the mandate from God to continue to feed those who cannot provide for themselves.

Quickly, the staff set about the task of completing the vegetable processing plant. They had been commissioned, by Wally, to finish the construction and begin the dehydration of vegetables. The next year was spent in erecting the steel building and outfitting it with equipment and electrical services. Staff rooms, spaces for storage, and a future lab for testing food quality, were built inside the large steel structure.

A transition was occurring within the ministry of Gleanings for the Hungry. For the first seventeen years, the sole food product produced was dried peaches and nectarines. From 1998 to December 2006, the California Raisin Growers generously donated over fourteen million pounds of raisins to the ministry of Gleanings for the Hungry. In addition, Lions Raisins, of Selma, California, demonstrated their generosity by processing, packaging, and even loading sea-going containers at their facility. The California Raisin Growers remain significant partners in the adventure; Gleanings is simply a conduit to get this nutritious food to the needy of the nations.

Ron and Shirley Wagner from Saskatoon, Canada, joined the Gleanings staff in 1999 (working previously as Gleanings Mission Builders). Utilizing his extensive sales background, Ron soon was able to acquire a variety of food products. In December 1998, 97,000 pounds of prunes were given for distribution; soon there would be dozens of products given to feed the poor. (See appendix for a schedule of products shipped in recent years).

With an increase in variety and quantity of products, Gleanings was able to partner with many more ministries to distribute the food. From the beginning of 1982 until 2007, Gleanings for the Hungry shipped an excess of twenty-six million pounds of food products to over eighty countries. The food was distributed by dozens of missions agencies and partnering churches.

Indeed Gleanings had become the "Joseph" ministry, acquiring food from the land of plenty, the United

States and sharing it with the impoverished around the world. Here is a sampling of excerpts from foreign missionaries:

Mongolia: We rejoice in knowing that because of you and your willingness to help, there are literally hundreds of children alive today.

Romania: If it were not for people like yourselves I would not be able to carry out the work the Lord has called my family to. Tomorrow hundreds of children will be eating thanks to your teams' efforts.

Armenia: Gleanings for the Hungry has brought to our people a new dimension of hope which is part of a vital process in reaching out to the spiritual needs of this impoverished land.

Moldova: In the name of thousands and thousands of orphans, poor families from Moldova and even Romania, I want to thank all of you who support the work of Gleanings. It is with your support and generosity that so many people and children from the Republic of Moldova survive throughout the year. With Gleanings as a faithful partner, we are able to do what even the government of Moldova cannot do for the children in State orphanages and the impoverished elderly. To God Be the Glory!

The Gleanings staff have always felt that their role was to be servants to other ministries. By working hard to provide food, they could enable missionaries and Christian workers to reach out with both hands of the gospel: the message of a Savior who loved and died for the sins of all mankind and the practical demonstration of God's care shown through the tangible provision of food.

Often the story was told of a team of missionaries witnessing to a very poor African villager. The elderly man listened respectively as the young men shared of the saving grace available through Jesus. When they finished their message, they asked if he had any questions. His reply was, "I'm sorry I really couldn't hear you, I am too hungry." His response has etched itself on the hearts and minds of everyone at Gleanings, staff and short-term volunteers alike. We have been given a mandate by the Lord Himself when He communicated to His followers, "What you did for one of the least of these brothers of mine, you did it for me" (Matt 25.40).

Some have inquired regarding the effectiveness of combining food distribution with evangelism. Perhaps, we see modeled the responsiveness of human nature as Jesus fed the multitudes. Following that miraculous provision, the crowds lobbied to make Him King! Although Gleanings does not directly link food distribution with forced evangelism, the message is clear: our God is a loving God and He cares deeply about peoples' needs. As to the question of evangelistic effectiveness, listen to this March 2004 testimonial:

> Feed The Hungry shipped eight, forty-foot containers to four different ministries in India. In the containers was a wide assortment of

high quality food and raisins (donated to Gleanings) that were divided up in each of the eight containers so that many received part of this wonderful blessing. The most exciting part was the number of people that came to know our Lord and Savior Jesus Christ. We have documented over 125,000 salvations because of a small key that opens big doors for the gospel and that key is called food. Everywhere we go the food is given and the gospel is preached. (Spirit/Soul/Body). On behalf of all the Lesea Global Feed the Hungry staff, we would like to thank you for all that you have done and are doing for the kingdom of God.

One of Wally Wenge's greatest dreams was the production of dehydrated vegetables. Although he did not live to see his dream fulfilled, in one short year God answered his prayers. Through the hard work of Ron Wagner and others, donations of *already dried* vegetables were received. These vegetables were mechanically air dried and made excellent components of an easy to reconstitute soup. The receipt of these products, coupled with the absence of fresh cull carrots (these were now being utilized in other ways) demonstrated clear guidance for the Gleanings folks: they could blend these products into a nutritious soup mix. A decision was made late in 1999 that shaped the future of the Gleanings ministry. With faith and vision they determined to pursue the production of a dehydrated soup mix utilizing donated dried vegetables, protein products (mostly soy based), and spices. Early in 2000, the first donations of soup products arrived and the adventure began.

Using amazing ingenuinity, John Nugier converted a cement mixer into a food blender. The vegetables were measured into the mixer and spun to thoroughly blend. The blended vegetable mix was then dumped into totes. Ralph Konkol used his extraordinary design and construction skills to assemble a simple conveyor belt. The dehydrated vegetables were placed on the conveyor, one cupful at a time in measured, spaced piles. Protein products and spices were added to each scoop of dried vegetables. The ever moving belt carried the completed product to a volunteer worker with a waiting plastic bag. The soup mix dropped off the end of the conveyor, into the bag, to eventually be placed into barrels for shipping. The process was simple, but it worked!

The timing of God is always perfect! Key people lent their expertise to assist in the development of this new product line. Mario Defrancesco owned a family business in California. Their specialty was the dehydration of garlic, onions, parsley and other spices. Mario strongly urged Gleanings to avoid the actual dehydration of vegetables, thus avoiding the high production costs and the necessary purchase of expensive lab equipment. His wise counsel steered the ministry into the appropriate direction. The generous donation of spices from Mario's company has seasoned the soup of millions of hungry people.

A loving Montana family, Dan and Patty Magalsky, heard of the inspiring work of Gleanings. Coming initially as short-term volunteers in November 2000, they eventually became the vegetable plant managers in 2001. Utilizing the pioneering work of others, they experimented with the soup mix by blending the vegetables, adding spices, soy-based protein products, and a variety of other items including lentils and macaroni. Dan and Patty pioneered the recipes (taste-testing each recipe themselves!) and developed the simple assembly line used in the first season (2000–2001). Eight thousand pounds of donated dehydrated vegetables were used in this inaugural season, resulting in 160,000 eight-ounce servings.

Over the next few years, additional products were acquired and machinery was installed. A state of the art vacuum system was used to lift the various soup components into a blender. Each large tote of individual products was placed on a scale so that accurate amounts would be vacuumed into the blender. After blending, volunteers, many of them retirees looking for an opportunity to serve, package the blended soup mix into one gallon plastic bags. When reconstituted, each package will make ten gallons of delicious soup, providing 100 times eight-ounce servings!

Increased product donation and improved mechanization enabled Dan, Patty, and their army of volunteers to dramatically increase production. The opening of "soup season" in 2005 saw a total of 740,000 eight-ounce servings of soup packaged. Three quarters of a million people were lovingly provided a hot meal in the name of Jesus! Even more amazing was the stunning announcement that five million eight-ounce servings were packaged in the first fourteen weeks of 2005! By the seventh season (2007) a total of 9,007,000 servings were packaged by compassionate volunteers. The projection is that the 2008 yield will be in excess of twenty million servings!

There are dozens of heart-touching testimonials documenting the significant value of the soup. In 2003 staff members Dave Romero and Tom Magalsky went to Africa to assist "Hearts of Compassion Ministry" hand out Gleanings food. They visited a school and reported this:

> ...the teachers saw the kids drinking a lot of water and questioned them. The kids said they had no food at home and they drink water to fill their stomachs. These kids, who now get food at school, when Friday comes they receive their last meal until Monday. The children gathered together and said, "Thank you for the soup mix." It was overwhelming when they thanked us in a big group; hundreds of children swarmed me because they wanted to shake my hand and thank me.

Story after story, each one tells the miracle of God's love and bears the wonder of God's touch. Perhaps the most amazing story of all was told by the group from Apple Creek Ministries, in Atascadero, who in 2004 distributed Gleanings soup mix in Zambia:

Our home base was an orphanage of Aid's victims. Our experience with feeding the poor was amazing. We filled several duffle bags full of the precious lentils and rice in the zip lock bags, along with some clothes and Bibles we intended to distribute. This food was so blessed, because no matter how much we cooked, regardless of how many people were served, there was always enough! This was truly a fishes and loaves experience. We gave as much food as fast as we could for a month, and it never ran out. The day we left we reached down to the bottom of the last duffle bag and pulled out the remaining bag. We knew exactly what to do with it. And it was over. How can we ever describe what a blessing the fruit of your labors have been to us and countless people that were touched by the hand of God through your ministry? With this note we send our heartfelt thanks for your gift of love that was given and received in the name of our Lord Jesus.

The remarkable growth of the ministry, both in scope and volume of product, can only be described as miraculous. Indeed, the passing of the founder, Wally Wenge, did not mean the end of Gleanings, rather a new beginning.

...but if it dies, it produces many seeds (John 12.24b).

A Photographic Journey

Diane Williams, Cathy Nehf, and Norma Wenge
working the first fruit line.

Norma, Wally (age 56), Rodkey (age 15) and Rodkey's mother pose
before leaving on the first fund-raising trip.

Norma Wenge (far right) cooked for all of the volunteers from a two-burner stove in the small trailer. Wally is seated second from the left.

Norma and Wally at the newly acquired Sultana property.

*Early on, Steve and Becky Witmer brought these Discipleship
Training School students to help. Steve, standing far left.
Becky, kneeling second from left.*

This sign is prominently posted at the Gleanings' facility.

1989: An 8-unit motel was built on the property to house volunteers.

*Wally and Norma show off the end product:
a bucket of dehydrated fruit.*

Wally and Loren Cunningham (founder of Youth With A Mission) at the Dedication of Gleanings For The Hungry.

Volunteers finish concrete on the vegetable soup facility.

Len (above) and Lois (below) Nylin
served as Gleanings Directors for
five and a half years after Wally's death.

Lois Nylin

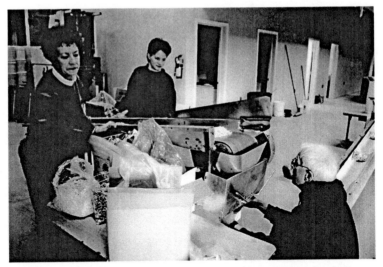

Veggie-soup beginnings: Ralph Konkol, right, built this simple line. Shirley Wagner, left, and Mary Chester try out the system.

Web Bamford (age 89), right, along with his friends built 7,000 fruit-dehydrating trays over a period of six years.

Volunteers repair bins used to haul fruit to Gleanings.

Early '90s: Connie and Eliot Henderson and two of their children, Lauren and Stephanie.

2000: Dave and Candy Romero and their children, Joel, Micah, Ezra, Charity. Dave and Levi. Candi and Josiah.

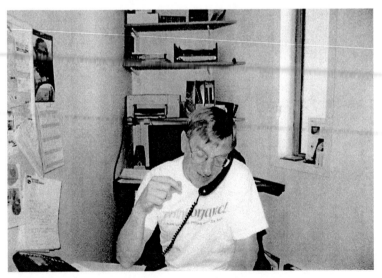

Ron Wagner, procurement.

Gleanings' property in the beginning.

Wally sorrounded by trays of dehydrating fruit.

CHAPTER 10
A MIRACLE OF MERCY

He who oppresses the poor shows contempt for their Maker, but whoever is kind to the needy honors God. Proverbs 14.31

In 2004, we saw many changes occur at Gleanings. Increased productivity meant that more volunteers were needed to man the production equipment. By the end of summer of that year, over 1,000 youth and leaders volunteered to serve on the fruit lines. Gleanings was becoming a destination of choice for church youth teams interested in a mercy-ministry-style outreach.

Weekly new recruits arrive, work zealously, transform the fruit of the valley into life-giving food for the impoverished and needy. Each weekday morning starts with a time of worship, prayer, and a devotional from a staff member or team leader. The true focus is always highlighted: "Our service shows God's love to the poor." Many youth find this experience to be transformational; deepening their personal walk with the Lord, and giving them a touch of God's heart for mercy and justice.

It was into this youth-filled environment that God brought the perfect couple to provide oversight to the Gleanings Ministry. Rick and Lynn O'Dwyer, serving as short-term staff at Gleanings, sensed the call of God to step into the roles of Director and wife. Leaving their ranch in Dawson Creek, BC, Canada, they made the transition to Sultana, California. Their unique giftings and life experience had shaped them for this season of service. Rick was a blend of Pastor/Administrator and Lynn had a delightful gift of hospitality with a remarkable creative flair. Together they make each volunteer feel welcomed and affirmed.

Stepping into his new role as Director in May 2004, Rick had just weeks to prepare for the summers' weekly influx of youth. It was an excellent year, with record amounts of fruit being processed. Drawing from his expertise in church leadership, Rick ensured that each young volunteer went away with a clear understanding of God's redeeming love and a true sense of appreciation for their selfless service.

These few short years were filled with global calamity; and Gleanings was able to respond quickly to the emergency situations. Food was shipped to alleviate the desperate needs of the Asian Christmas Tsunami disaster of 2004. Earthquakes, hurricane Katrina, devastating drought in Somalia, civil war in Sudan, each situation was critical. Faithfully, Rick, Lynn, and their dedicated team addressed the many needs presented to them. With the expansion of the ministry, so too did the desperate opportunities. As with Esther, it seemed they "had come to the Kingdom for such a time as this."

During the first five years of Gleanings existence, the bulk of dried fruit was shipped to the Cambodian refugee camps, mostly located in Thailand. Deeply impacted by their experience in caring for these devastated peoples, Wally and Norma Wenge dedicated themselves and the ministry, to attempt to alleviate their hunger and suffering. Eventually the camps were all closed and the refugees were repatriated with the help of the U.N. and other benevolent organizations.

Time passed and the world's focus shifted to other countries and new calamities. The Cambodians, victimized by the brutality of the Pol Pot regime, continued to experience daily terror and difficulties. Most villagers returned to the charred remains of their homes. Their hastily left household goods were either stolen or destroyed by fire. Yet terror remained in the form of countless numbers of land mines. Annually tens of thousands are maimed or killed by these brutal reminders of an unjust war.

Cambodia was a nation deeply scarred, disheartened, and desperate for a message of hope. Foursquare missionary couple Ted and Sue Olbrich were deployed to plant churches and evangelize in this predominantly Buddhist nation. Just weeks into their tenure, they would experience a Divine intrusion that would forever change the face of Cambodia and open a new partnership between Gleanings for the Hungry and the Cambodian people.

Early one morning, Ted Olbrich heard a knock at his door. Standing there was a Cambodian man holding a small child. Knowing very little Cambodian, communicating was difficult, but Ted realized that the child was an orphan and the child was being given to him! Ted attempted to explain that he was a missionary and church planter and they did not have an orphanage. In one convincing statement the Cambodian gentleman said, "Aren't you a Christian?" to which Ted replied, "Yes, of course." Then, he queried, "Isn't that what Christians do: take care of orphans?"

Ted found himself soon in the custody of several orphan children. He visited every orphanage in the area and found they were overcrowded; some begged him to take some of their children! Within a short time, Ted and Sue had a full house with twenty-five orphan children. What seemed to be an intrusion into their plans was actually God's intervention. It was this act of kindness that opened the door into people's hearts. The revelation of a God of love and mercy was cool water on the disheartened souls of the Cambodian people. Seeing the care given to the "least of these," the orphan children, communities opened their hearts to the good news of the gospel.

A season of rapid church growth occurred, albeit using an unusual strategy: start a children's home to care for orphans, employ Christian widows to live with and provide the mothering care these children needed. A Church would be started, discipling the newly evangelized converts. The power of the Lord accompanied their efforts with supernatural demonstrations of healing and signs and wonders attesting the greatness of God.

The work grew to staggering proportion; by mid 2005, Ted and Sue and their team were caring for 3,500 orphans and 500 widows serving as caretakers. These beautiful children, and the ministry created to care for them was called "Foursquare Children of Promise." Remarkable stories always require extraordinary faith challenges and Ted's challenge was to feed 4,000 widows and orphans each day. When the government announced that they would be dramatically cutting the rice quota, the need became critical.

Through a network of friendships, the Cambodian need became known to Gleanings for the Hungry. Regular shipments of rice, soup mix, fruit, raisins, and other nutritious products have served to supplement their diet. Currently, an average of one forty-foot container of food is shipped each month to aid the Foursquare Children of Promise!

The Cambodian people and their needs were so instrumental in formulating the initial vision for Gleanings, that it is only fitting that they are substantial recipients of the Gleanings products. The circle of mercy is complete! These precious ones who captured the hearts of Wally and Norma Wenge are being lovingly cared for through this partnership of Gleanings and the Foursquare Children of Promise.

Perhaps Norma Wenge said it best in her March 2004 letter to Gleanings' donors:

> In 1980, Wally and I went to Thailand to work in the refugee camps for the Cambodians fleeing the terror of the evil regime of Pol Pot. Our hearts were broken with the stories of all they and theirs endured. We knew God was impressing on our hearts to help the poor and needy. But how?
>
> In 1981, we were in the San Joaquin Valley and saw the waste of good fruit lying between the rows of trees to rot. Christmas of 1981 was spent at our daughter's home. During our quiet time, in the book of Ruth we read how she gleaned the fields of Boaz. The understanding came to us! The fruit of the Valley was being thrown away or at best fed to cattle. This would be the gleanings of the Valley! We pursued this and through God's chosen people, we had our first fruit season For five years, the fruit was shipped to the refugees. God led us where we now have Gleanings and God has blessed and blessed many in great need.
>
> Last month the leaders of the Canada team shared with me and I am still blessed and in awe of what God is doing through this ministry. Eleven people in four and a half days bagged enough soup to feed 528,000 hungry

orphans and widows and guess where? Yes, in Cambodia. The Foursquare Church has eighty orphanages. While the Canadians were here, two containers were loaded, one with all soup mix and the other with fruit, energy bars, and much more. We were informed that the orphanages had only one-month supply of food and were searching for more. Through God's divine appointment, the need found Gleanings, and the loaded containers were prayed over and were on their way to meet these needs. This group of mission builders are from the Foursquare Church, so you know how blessed and excited they were to have this privilege. All glory be to God our Father and Our Lord Jesus Christ. When God's people work in unity, much can be accomplished. Thank you, Steve and Barry Witmer, for having God's mercy heart.

What is so amazing is that the care being provided is physical (food), emotional (loving care), and spiritual (the gospel is presented). The Kingdom of God is advancing through the preaching of the gospel and the care of orphans. Most importantly, in all that is done God is most gloriously honored.

...but whoever is kind to the needy honors God... Proverbs 14.31.

CHAPTER 11
THE UNFINISHED STORY

God is not unjust; He will not forget your work and
the love you have shown Him as you have helped His people
and continue to help them. Hebrews 6.10

The story of Gleanings continues to be written with the pen of God's divine purpose. In amazement, we watch his unfolding plan. Weekly there are new opportunities, critical needs somewhere in the world, and the loving volunteers to help us meet these needs.

The staff and volunteers are the true heroes in this story. They come from a wide variety of backgrounds, ethnicities, and ages. From our oldest volunteer, Web Bamber, who began volunteering at eighty-eight years of age and continued beyond his ninety-fourth birthday, to homeschooled children assisting their parents in packaging soup mix, each person is essential and a tremendous blessing.

Together, young and old, men and women share the common understanding that serving at Gleanings helps to fulfill the scriptural command found in James 1.27: "Religion that God our Father accepts as pure and faultless is this: to look after widows and orphans in their distress and to keep oneself from being polluted by the world."

Annually, Gleanings exports two primary products. The first is obvious; it is the food shipped everywhere to alleviate suffering. The second export is not so tangibly perceived, but every bit as powerful. This "export" is the deposit of God's heart for the needy, placed in every volunteer who serves. Each one goes home changed, having been impacted by a God of mercy and challenged to reach out to those He greatly loves. When we truly understand God's heart, His broken heart for the poor, the orphan, and the widow, we are motivated to act mercifully as well. Perhaps the old cliché really is true: "Like Father, like Son." May we all become increasingly like Jesus, our model for true mercy and champion for justice.

The story of Gleanings is a journey, and we have not arrived at our destination. Would you walk beside us on this next stage of our travels? Ours is an unfinished story. Perhaps God would like to write you into the script as He completes the next chapter. We would delightfully embrace your participation! As we view the content of the previous chapters, we can say with faith-filled certainty that this next chapter will be amazing! See you soon.

"We always thank God for all of you, mentioning you in our prayers. We continually remember before our God and Father your work produced by faith, your labor prompted by love, and your endurance inspired by hope in our Lord Jesus Christ" (1 Thess 1.1-3).

For more information, please contact:

Gleanings for the Hungry

PO Box 309

Sultana, CA 93618

Phone: 559.591.5009

Fax: 559.591.5036

Email: info@gleanings.org

Web: www.gleanings.org

S cripture clearly communicates the power of unity in Psalms 133.1–3:

> How good and pleasant it is when brethren live together in unity!
> It is like precious oil poured on the head, running down the beard,
> running down on Aaron's beard, down upon the collar of his robes.
> It is as if the dew of Hebron were falling on Mount Zion.
> For there the Lord bestows his blessing even life forever more.

Gleanings for the Hungry provides almost daily testimonials and living proof of the truth of this passage. Partnering with dozens of ministries who gratefully receive and distribute the product, they continue to see God's favor and bestowed blessing. Everyday miracles, in the form of answered prayer, cause us to rejoice in God's provision and grant us faith to continually stretch ahead in this mission of compassion.

What follows is a simple spreadsheet outlining the ministries receiving Gleanings food, the types of food shipped, and the weight. I trust you won't see this simply as a table of meaningless data, but rather view these pages as an amazing testimonial to the faithfulness of our loving Father's ability to provide!

Secondly, as you read, please pray for these ministries and the men and women who lead them. These precious members of our eternal family are on the front lines of ministry. Their hands are the hands of Jesus, loving, caring, and serving — "the least of these my brothers."

Unity. Serving together with many ministry partners is the spiritual DNA of Gleanings for the Hungry. God's promise is to grace our unity and cooperation with His blessing. The following pages are a demonstration of God's favor and richest blessings.

Gleanings for the Hungry — Product Shipped 2006

Date	Organization	Country	Product
12-Jan	Church of Glad Tidings	Cambodia	cooking oil, energy bars
16-Jan	Spring of Life	Mexico	beans
18-Jan	Convoy of Hope	U. S., Netherlands, Philippines	pasta, seasoned flour
18-Jan	Feed The Hungry	U.S.	balanced carb drinks
24-Jan	Spring of Life	Mexico	dried fruit, energy bars, muffin mix, flour, beans

30-Jan	Operation Blessing	Ukraine	raisins
3-Feb	Night Shift Ministries	Canada	beans, onions, potatoes, coconut, trail mix, freeze dried corn, pasta, dried fruit
6-Feb	Children's Hunger Fund	Peru, Mexico	beans, flour, muffin mix, bars, fruit
15-Feb	Christian Aid Ministries	various countries	raisins
17-Feb	Beth Messiah Humanitarian Aid Ministry	Belarus	raisins, beans, dried fruit
23-Feb	Foundation For His Ministry	Mexico	dried fruit, raisins, noodles, strawberry fines
23-Feb	North Fresno Church	Mexico	peaches, beans, almonds, raisins
7-Mar	Children's Hunger Fund	various countries	lima beans, freeze dried strawberry powder
17-Mar	Gateway Bible--Santa Cruz	Mexico	banberra beans
20-Mar	Threshold Ministries	China	raisins, dried fruit
21-Mar	YWAM--Latvia	Latvia	raisins, beans, dried fruit, trail mix
23-Mar	Convoy of Hope	U.S.	pasta, croutons
29-Mar	Operation Blessing	U.S.	frozen apples, frozen cherries
6-Apr	Spring of Life	Mexico	dried tom., beans, dried fruit, straw., trail mix, nacho seasoning
7-Apr	Church of Glad Tidings	Cambodia	dried soup mix

The Best Kept Secret in YWAM!

10-Apr	Convoy of Hope	U.S.	water, pasta sauce
12-Apr	Convoy of Hope	U.S.	ginger bread mix
14-Apr	Convoy of Hope	Netherlands, El Salvador, Cambodia, Philippines, Jamaica, Dominican Republic,	dried soup mix
14-Apr	Father's Heart International	Zambia	dried soup mix
21-Apr	Armenian Gospel Mission	Armenia	raisins, dried fruit, trail mix, soup mix, beans
26-Apr	Convoy of Hope	various countries	rice, water, vitamins
26-Apr	Children's Hunger Relief Fund	South Africa	raisins, dried soup mix
28-Apr	Children's Hunger Fund	United States	salsa, green taco sauce
28-Apr	Dream Center	United States	salsa, green taco sauce
2-May	Convoy of Hope	Lithuania	rice
5-May	CTW/Change The World	Mongolia	raisins, dried fruit, soup mix, straw, dried fruit, raisins, soup mix, straw, dried pepper powder, almonds, dried tomatoes, apple chips,
16-May	Last Harvest Ministries	Mexico	dried fruit, healthy handfuls, freeze dried strawberries, dried carrot, pasta, soy, mangos

114

17-May	Armenian Gospel Mission	Armenia	raisins, dried fruit, soup mix, straw.
22-May	Convoy of Hope	United States	water
23-May	Christian Aid Ministries	various countries	soup mix, tomato and pasta blend, trail mix, straw. fines
24-May	Foursquare Children of Promise	Cambodia	soup mix, energy bars, healthy handfuls, beans
25-May	Convoy of Hope	Indonesia	soup mix
31-May	Children's Hunger Fund	various countries	soup mix, healthy handfuls
6-Jun	Gain	Ukraine	raisins, fruit, beans, strawberries
12-Jun	The Church of Bible Understanding	Haiti	soup mix, beans, yellow peas, dried tomatoes, freeze dried strawberries
19-Jun	Jimmy Hughs Ministry	Honduras	soup, dried tomatoes, beans
21-Jun	Last Harvest Ministries	Mexico	healthy handfuls, dried fruit, infused raisins, chocolate covered seeds
29-Jun	Armenian Gospel Mission	Armenia	soup, oats, dried fruit, strawberries
29-Jun	Indonesian Relief Fund	Indonesia	raisins, trail mix
26-Jul	Christian Aid Ministries	various countries	raisins
26-Jul	Church of Glad Tidings	Cambodia	cooking oil
26-Jul	Dream Center	United States	cooking oil

26-Jul	Convoy of Hope	Honduras, Suriname, Haiti, Guatemala, Nicaragua, Jamaica	raisins
26-Jul	Children's Hunger Fund	Mexico, U.S.	peas, beans, healthy handfuls
1-Aug	Last Harvest Ministries	Mexico	raisins, flour, cashews, cherry raisins, salsa
1-Aug	Churches of Christ Disaster Relief	United States	dried fruit
4-Aug	Operation Blessing	United States	salsa, green taco sauce
7-Aug	Church of Glad Tidings	Cambodia	raisins
8-Aug	Dream Center	United States	spices, pasta, etc.
8-Aug	Children's Hunger Fund	United States	salsa, green taco sauce
10-Aug	Operation Blessing International	Romania	raisins
17-Aug	Convoy of Hope	United States	salsa, green taco sauce
17-Aug	Last Harvest Ministries	Mexico	nuts, dried oranges, choc. covered seeds, dried fruit, soup, oat cups
17-Aug	Foursquare Children of Promise	Cambodia	almonds, soup and oat cups, dried fruit
18-Aug	Foundation For His Ministry	Mexico	raisins, kandi kernels, trail mix, dried fruit, salsa, oats
19-Aug	Convoy of Hope	United States	butter spray

23-Aug	Convoy of Hope	United States	water
24-Aug	Wheat Mission Assoc. in America	North Korea	raisins, soup, dried fruit
25-Aug	Last Harvest Ministries	Mexico	dried fruit, dried persimmons, kandi kernels
28-Aug	Feed The Hungry Lesea	various countries	raisins
31-Aug	Convoy of Hope	various countries	raisins
31-Aug	Operation Blessing	Guatemala, Ukraine	raisins
2-Sep	Convoy of Hope	various countries	dried fruit
10-Sep	Father's Heart International	Zambia	raisins, beans, rice, pasta, oats, dried fruit
14-Sep	Children's Hunger Fund	Eastern Europe	raisins
25-Sep	Feed The Hungry Lesea	Haiti	raisins
26-Sep	Childcare World Wide	Peru	raisins
26-Sep	Hi Mission	Mexico	dried fruit and variety food products
29-Sep	Osborne Indian Mission	United States	dried fruit
3-Oct	Last Harvest Ministries	Mexico	dried fruit, kandi kernels, chips, drinks
3-Oct	Vineyard Church Selma	United States, Mexico	flour, drinks
13-Oct	Children's Hunger Fund	United States	coffee drinks
13-Oct	Operation Blessing	United States	coffee drinks
13-Oct	Convoy of Hope	United States	beans

16-Oct	Foundation For His Ministry	Mexico	baby food
17-Oct	Children's Hunger Fund	various countries	dried fruit, salsa, taco sauce, baby food
18-Oct	Armenian Gospel Mission	Armenia	raisins, dried fruit
18-Oct	Food For The Poor	Nicaragua, Jamaica, Trinidad, Guatemala, Dominican Republic, Honduras, Belize, El Salvador, Haiti	raisins
2-Nov	Universal Aid	Romania	raisins
3-Nov	Hearts of Compassion	Mexico	dried fruit, energy bars, freeze dried strawberries
3-Nov	Convoy of Hope	Panama	raisins, dried fruit
3-Nov	Last Harvest Ministries	Mexico	choc. sunflower seeds, energy bars
9-Nov	Christian Aid Ministries	various countries	raisins
9-Nov	Convoy of Hope	United States	pasta, millet flour, wheat germ with cinnamon and flax
15-Nov	Church of Glad Tidings	Cambodia	soup, cooking oil, strawberries, energy bars, rice bowls, coconut milk
16-Nov	Beth Messiah Humanitarian Aid Ministry	Belarus	raisins, dried fruit
27-Nov	Last Harvest Ministries	Mexico	drinks, chips, nuts

1-Dec	Ahead Ministries	Liberia	raisins, soup, beans
5-Dec	Container Ministry	South Africa	soup mix
5-Dec	Children's Hunger Fund	various countries	soup mix
6-Dec	YWAM--Arizona	United States	dried fruit
6-Dec	Church of Glad Tidings	Cambodia	soup mix, Mrs. May's Naturals--sunflower snacks, children's vitamins
7-Dec	Feed The Children	Nicaragua, Guatemala, El Salvador, Honduras, Philippines	raisins
7-Dec	Jimmy Hughes Ministry	Honduras, Mexico	raisins, dried fruit, Hansen beverages
7-Dec	Osborne Indian Mission	United States	dried fruit
11-Dec	The Container Ministry	South Africa	raisins
12-Dec	Feed The Children	United States	tortillas
12-Dec	Operation Blessing	United States	tortillas
12-Dec	Convoy of Hope	United States	tortillas
13-Dec	Convoy of Hope	various countries	raisins, dried soup mix
13-Dec	Christian In Action, Inc.	Columbia	dried fruit, chips, drinks
14-Dec	Jimmy Hughes Ministry	Mexico	raisins, dried fruit, Hansen beverages
17-Dec	Gateway Bible--Santa Cruz	Mexico	raisins, dried fruit, pasta
19-Dec	Father's Heart International	Zambia	raisins, dried fruit

| 20-Dec | Church of Glad Tidings | Cambodia | raisins |
| 27-Dec | Armenian Gospel Mission | Armenia | raisins |

Total Product Shipped In 2006 ~ 3,945,328 Lbs

Gleanings for the Hungry — Product Shipped 2007

Date	Organization	Country	Product
7-Jan	Christian Aid Ministries	Various countries	raisins
10-Jan	First Baptist Modesto	United States	dried fruit
10-Jan	Last Harvest Ministries	Mexico	dried fruit, soup
10-Jan	Dream Center	United States	cooking oil
11-Jan	Agape Manna Inc.	North Korea	raisins
12-Jan	Foursquare Children of Promise	Cambodia	cooking oil
17-Jan	Bethlehem Project	North Korea	raisins
19-Jan	Children's Hunger Fund	United States, various countries	raisins, pasta
24-Jan	Cornerstone Church	United States	pasta, salsa
25-Jan	Last Harvest Ministries	Mexico	pasta, glaced fruit, coconut milk

25-Jan	Convoy of Hope	Nicaragua, El Salvador, Honduras, Domican Republic, Mexico, Ghana, Nauru (Island in the South Pacific),Tajikistan, Jamaica (dried fruit), Panama, Netherlands (soup), Peru(soup mix), Haiti (dried fruit), Philippines (soup, dried fruit),	raisins, dried fruit, soup
31-Jan	Convoy of Hope	United States	soy milk
6-Feb	Last Harvest Ministries	Mexico	dried fruit, glaced fruit
15-Feb	Global Aid Network	Georgia	raisins, dried fruit
16-Feb	Feed The Children	United States	baby food
17-Feb	Convoy of Hope	Various countries	raisins
21-Feb	Ahead Ministries	Liberia	oatmeal, dried soup
22-Feb	Armenian Gospel Mission	Armenia	whole wheat flour
23-Feb	Cram Worldwide	North Korea	raisins
2-Mar	Church of Glad Tidings	Cambodia	soup
2-Mar	Armenian Gospel Mission	Armenia	raisins, oat flour, wheat flour
7-Mar	Reach Now International, Inc.	Mozambique	raisins, soup, dried fruit, glazed fruit
12-Mar	Dream Center	United States	chili sauce
13-Mar	Gateway Bible Church	Mexico	coconut milk, variety Asian noodles

22-Mar	Last Harvest Ministries	Mexico	rice, chili sauce, dried fruit, Asian noodles
28-Mar	Fraser Valley Gleaners	Paraguay, Sudan, Nigeria, Romania, Guatemala	bars
30-Mar	Foundation For His Ministry	Mexico	trail mix, salsa, figs, thai drinks, thai food, rice cakes
30-Mar	Kathy Howard Music Ministries	Mexico	thai food
3-Apr	Last Harvest Ministries	Mexico	salsa, dried fruit, dried apples, thai iced tea
3-Apr	Church of Glad Tidings	Cambodia	soup mix, cooking oil
4-Apr	Children's Hunger Fund	El Salvador	soup mix, dried fruit
10-Apr	Foundation For His Ministry	Mexico	bars
11-Apr	Fiji Foursquare Church	Fiji	raisins, dried fruit, soup mix, candy
17-Apr	Hugo Ministries	Mexico	dried fruit
4-May	Grace Fellowship Foursquare Church	El Salvador	dried fruit, trail mix, soup mix
4-May	Cornerstone Church	United States	salsa, chili sauce
9-May	Convoy of Hope	El Salvador	cereal
11-May	Children's Hunger Fund	United States	soy milk
21-May	Dream Center	United States	non-dairy creamer
23-May	Dasom Church	North Korea	dried soup mix
29-May	Church of Glad Tidings	Cambodia	raisins, dried fruit

6-Jun	Convoy of Hope	El Salvador	dried fruit, soup mix
15-Jun	Last Harvest Ministries	Mexico	dried fruit, trail mix, flour, jumbo raisins, soup mix,
13-Jul	Little Samaritan Mission	Moldova	dried fruit
17-Jul	Children's Hunger Fund	United States	Jiffy mixes
20-Jul	Reach Now International, Inc.	Zambia	dried fruit, soup mix
23-Jul	Kingsway Charities Benevolent Fund	United States	strawberry puree cubes
2-Aug	Convoy of Hope	Peru, Nicaragua, Mexico, Haiti, Zimbabwe, Jamaica	dried fruit, soup mix, cornbread, flour, soy protein powder, soy flour
10-Aug	Convoy of Hope	Mexico	salsa, taco sauce
18-Aug	Last Harvest Ministries	Mexico	dried fruit, trail mix, jumbo raisins, soy milk, chips
22-Aug	Church of Glad Tidings	Cambodia	dried fruit
23-Aug	Children's Hunger Fund	Peru	dried fruit, soup mix
28-Aug	Little Samaritan Mission	Moldova	dried fruit, soup mix, jumbo raisins
31-Aug	Reach Now International, Inc.	Zimbabwe	dried fruit, soup mix
31-Aug	Cornerstone Church	United States	sugar, tea
5-Sep	The Container Ministry	South Africa	dried fruit, soup mix
6-Sep	Operation Blessing International	Peru	dried fruit

The Best Kept Secret in YWAM!

13-Sep	Child Life International	Romania	dried fruit
20-Sep	Foundation For His Ministry	Mexico	dried fruit, raisins, soup, protein, cheese sauce
27-Sep	Dream Center	United States	fruit tea
27-Sep	Feed The Children	United States	fruit tea
4-Oct	Dream Center	United States	flour, seasonings, jumbo raisins
11-Oct	Peoples Church	Jordan	dried fruit
22-Oct	Little Samaritan Mission	Moldova	flour, dried fruit
26-Oct	Last Harvest Ministries	Mexico	mighty milk
26-Oct	Children's Hunger Fund	Mexico	mighty milk
30-Oct	Solona Beach Presbyterian Church	United States	raisins
31-Oct	Foundation For His Ministry	Mexico	dried fruit, soup
1-Nov	Last Harvest Ministries	Mexico	oatmeal, soups, flavoring, wheat and spelt flakes, cornmeal, spices
3-Nov	Dream Center	United States	frozen mixed vegetables
14-Nov	Gleanings for the Hungry	Guatemala	dried fruit, raisins, trail and nut mix
19-Nov	Last Harvest Ministries	Mexico	mighty milk, trail mix, soup mix, red bell pepper powder, oatmeal
27-Nov	Children's Hunger Fund	United States	spicy peanut sauce, noodles

124

29-Nov	Reach Now International, Inc.	Burkina Faso, Niger	dried fruit
29-Nov	Last Harvest Ministries	Mexico	pizza chips, dried fruit, dried oranges and persimmons
3-Dec	Dream Center	United States	sugar coated pecans
7-Dec	Global Response Team (Div. of IDT)	Liberia	dried fruit
17-Dec	Last Harvest Ministries	Mexico	dried pepper powder, pizza chips
20-Dec	Last Harvest Ministries	Mexico	mighty milk
20-Dec	Jimmy Hughes Ministries	Honduras	mighty milk, dried fruit
27-Dec	Little Samaritan Mission	Moldova	dried fruit

Total Product Shipped in 2007 — 3,202,022 lbs.

APPENDIX 2
PRODUCT DONATION

Gleanings for the Hungry has been remarkably blessed to have many businesses and corporations partner with us to feed the hungry. Their generous donations of food products have enabled us to greatly multiply our global impact. The listing which follows is not complete (perhaps in the early years we were too busy living the miracle to accurately document it!). It is simply a sampling of the great donors who have supported the mission with "gifts in kind."

To all of our donors, those identified and those unidentified, we honor you! Without you, we could not have accomplished our mission. While words of gratitude are inadequate to fully express our appreciation, we pray that the loving and eternal God, whom we serve, will shower His richest blessings upon you!

Gleanings for the Hungry Product Donation ~ 2006

Date	Name	Product
18-Jan	Hodgson Mill, Inc.	seasoned flour
18-Jan	Liberty Richter	balanced carb drinks
19-Jan	Van Drunen Farms	freeze dried chive, onion, dried fruit, freeze dried hash browns
27-Jan	De Francesco & Sons, Inc.	garlic, onions
30-Jan	American Italian Pasta Co.	pasta
16-Feb	Oregon Freeze Dry, Inc.	corn, freeze dried strawberry fines
21-Feb	Quick Dry Foods USA, Inc.	dried carrots, broccoli florets
28-Feb	Convoy of Hope	rice, pasta
1-Mar	Culinary Farms	dried tomatoes
1-Mar	Jones Produce Dehy	dehydrated potatoes
8-Mar	Orchard Valley Harvest	nuts, dried fruit
10-Mar	Far West Rice, Inc.	rice
17-Mar	Superior Quality Foods	gourmet crockery seasoning
23-Mar	Accurate Logistics	pasta, croutons
27-Mar	Pacific Farms	dried carrots
28-Mar	Oregon Freeze Dry, Inc.	frozen cherries
29-Mar	TreeTop	frozen apples
6-Apr	De Francesco & Sons, Inc.	garlic, onions, parsley
10-Apr	UNFI	water, pasta sauce
12-Apr	Brake Machinery	lentils, yellow peas
12-Apr	Hodgson Mill, Inc.	gingerbread mix
12-Apr	Healthy Times	baby food cereal
21-Apr	Far West Rice, Inc.	rice

24-Apr	UNFI	water, rice, vitamins
27-Apr	SK Foods	salsa, green taco sauce (cans)
28-Apr	Oregon Freeze Dry, Inc.	corn, strawberry and mango fines
2-May	Sun Valley Rice Company	rice
8-May	Premier Nutrition	energy bars
8-May	BioPharma Scientific, Inc.	Green food powders
11-May	Bob's Red Mill	rolled oats
12-May	Healthy Handfuls	healthy handfuls (cookies, crackers)
22-May	Convoy of Hope	rice, pasta, power aide
22-May	Convoy of Hope	water
6-Jun	Erker Grain Company	flavored raisins, chocolate covered sunflower seeds
12-Jun	SK Foods	salsa suprema medium (cans)
19-Jun	SK Foods	taco sauce, salsa, salsa green
20-Jun	Bella Viva Orchards	dried peaches and apricots
23-Jun	San Francisco Spice Co.	spices, seasoning mixes, soup, flavorings, pasta
13-Jul	Premier Nutrition	energy bars
13-Jul	Stone-Buhr Flour Company	flour
14-Jul	Oregon Freeze Dry, Inc.	freeze dried corn, freeze dried strawberry fines
17-Jul	SK Foods	taco sauce, salsa, salsa verde
18-Jul	ACH Food Companies Inc.	cooking oil
18-Jul	ACH Food Companies Inc.	butter spray
21-Jul	Convoy of Hope	power aide
1-Aug	International Trade Co., Inc.	soy protein, soy concentrate

3-Aug	Legacy Foods	TVP
4-Aug	SK Foods	salsa, green taco sauce
10-Aug	Kirsten Co. LLC	pinto beans
18-Aug	UNFI	water
9-Oct	Thai Kitchen	coconut milk, soup bowls
10-Oct	Genesee Union Warehouse	lentils
11-Oct	Initiative Foods	baby food
11-Oct	Initiative Foods	coffee drinks
13-Oct	NCW Alliance Bean & Grain	beans
16-Oct	Bunge Foods	cooking oil
18-Oct	Mercer Foods	freeze dried peas, freeze dried corn, diced red bell peppers, dried peaches
27-Oct	Freeze-Dry Foods, Inc.	dried tomatoes
1-Nov	Premier Pulses	lentils
1-Nov	RDO Processing	dried potatoes
2-Nov	Zerega Pasta	Pasta
7-Nov	De Francesco & Sons, Inc.	powdered parsley
7-Nov	Bella Viva Orchards	dried nectarines
8-Nov	G & R Foods	pasta, millet flour, wheat germ
20-Nov	UNFI	vitamins
22-Nov	De Francesco & Sons, Inc.	powdered parsley
28-Nov	De Francesco & Sons, Inc.	powdered parsley
29-Nov	De Francesco & Sons, Inc.	powdered parsley
30-Nov	Mrs. Mays	Mrs. May's Naturals sunflower crunch
4-Dec	Fine Dried Foods	dried mango and pineapple
5-Dec	Far West Rice, Inc.	rice
12-Dec	Oregon Freeze Dry, Inc.	flour
13-Dec	Adams Grain	wheat/flour

13-Dec	Ministry Partners	dried carrots
13-Dec	Mission Foods	tortillas
13-Dec	ARK Partnership	almonds
18-Dec	Simply Asia Foods, Inc.	soup bowls, coconut milk
27-Dec	Oregon Freeze Dry, Inc.	freeze dried corn, freeze dried bananas
31-Dec	RAC	raisins

Total Product Donated — 3,694,345 lbs.

Gleanings for the Hungry ~ Product Donation 2007

Date	Name	Product
8-Jan	International Glace, Inc.	glace fruit
8-Jan	Inland Empire Foods, Inc.	dehydrated. beans
9-Jan	Bunge Oils	cooking oils
10-Jan	ACH Foods	cooking oils, margarine
10-Jan	Convoy of Hope	pasta
12-Jan	Nutri-Pea Limited	pea fiber and protein
23-Jan	SK Foods	salsa
23-Jan	Superior Quality Foods	crockery seasoning
26-Jan	Bella Viva Orchards	dried fruit, nectarines, plums, figs
29-Jan	Mercer Processing, Inc.	freeze dried super sweet corn
31-Jan	Panos Brand	better than milk soymilk
1-Feb	Culinary Farms	variety of foodstuffs
5-Feb	Bob's Red Mill	10 grain bread mix
6-Feb	Far West Rice	rice
16-Feb	Initiative Foods, Inc.	baby food
16-Feb	Biopharma Scientific, Inc.	green powder
20-Feb	Dakota Dry Bean, Inc.	split yellow peas
23-Feb	Simply Asia Foods, Inc.	chili sauce, misc. food

27-Feb	FDP USA	variety dehydrated vegetables
8-Mar	Convoy of Hope	pasta
19-Mar	Lundberg Family Farms	rice cakes, rice
20-Mar	Sconza Candy Company	candies
23-Mar	Mercer Processing, Inc.	cauliflower, blueberries, peas, carrots, pineapple, strawberry
26-Mar	SK Foods	salsa
27-Mar	JM Grain	lentils
28-Mar	Bunge Oils	cooking oil
28-Mar	Creative Energy Food, Inc.	bars
10-Apr	Premier Nutrition	bars
27-Apr	SK Foods	salsa
4-May	Sensient Dehydrated	green beans, corn, veg. blend
7-May	Kikkoman	soymilk
9-May	UNFI	cereal
16-May	Heartland Ingredients	pasta
20-May	Ropak	plastic buckets
21-May	ACH Foods	non-dairy creamer
22-May	Mrs. May's	naturals crunch
25-May	Fresno Co-op	golden raisins
30 May	Kikkoman	soymilk
5-Jun	Northwest Natural Products	children's vitamins
12-Jun	Bob's Red Mill	variety of foodstuffs
18-Jun	Legacy Foods	TVP
17-Jul	Chelsea Milling Company	Jiffy mixes (pizza crust, brownie, pie crust, yellow cake, muffin, baking mix
23-Jul	Kellogg Company	strawberry

9-Aug	San Francisco Spice	spices and flavoring, chopped onions, pasta, diced potatoes
10-Aug	ConAgra	broccoli, cabbage cores, kraft variety blend, celery, grb granuals, protein powder, rice based protein powder, parsley powder, parsley powder, parsley/ spinach blend
10-Aug	ConAgra	sugar, parsley flakes
10-Aug	SK Foods	salsa, taco sauce
9-Sep	Heartland Ingredients	cinnamon cheerios
14-Sep	Inland Empire Foods, Inc.	dehydrated garbanzo whole, dehydrated pinto whole, dehydrated dk kidney flakes, dehydrated green pea flakes, dehydrated green northern whole, dehy navy flakes, dehy navy flour, dehy french gr lentil whole, white eye flour, raw green pea flour, pinto flakes, ultra soy tvp, spices, legumes, dehy peppers
27-Sep	ITO EN (North America), Inc.	fruit teas
27-Sep	ITO EN (North America), Inc.	fruit teas
2-Oct	Mario DeFrancesco	flour
3-Oct	Nurti-Pea Limited	pea fiber, pea protein
20-Oct	Indian Harvest	black beans precooked, red beans precooked
23-Oct	Fresno Co-op	jumbo golden raisins
26-Oct	Mareblu Naturals	trail mix and nut snacks

26-Oct	Cytosport	mighty milk
29-Oct	San Francisco Spice	flavorings, pasta, corn grits, wheat flakes, and oatmeal
30-Oct	North American Foods	dried potato flakes, dried potato diced, dried potato shreds, dried potato slices
30-Oct	ARK General Partnership	almonds
3-Nov	ConAgra	frozen mixed vegetables
14-Nov	Oregon Freeze Dry, Inc.	corn fines, pasta
15-Nov	Xengaru Fun Foods	pizzettos
20-Nov	Creative Energy Food, Inc.	raisins
20-Nov	Shoei Foods	toasted coconut
27-Nov	Mars Food	noodles, spicy peanut sauce
27-Nov	Far West Rice	rice
27-Nov	Chris Cardells	almonds
27-Nov	Bella Viva Orchards	misc. dried fruit
28-Nov	Devansoy, Inc.	soy flour
30-Nov	Far West Rice	rice
3-Dec	El Ruisenor de Mexico, Inc.	sugar coated pecans
3-Dec	Valley Harvest Nut Co. Inc.	almonds
27-Dec	RPAC	almonds
20-Dec	Cytosport	mighty milk

Total Product Donated in 2007 – 2,024,307 Lbs.

List of Countries Aided 2006–2007

Armenia	Belarus	Belize
Burkina Faso	Cambodia	Canada
China	Columbia	Dominican Republic
Eastern Europe	El Salvador	Fiji
Ghana	Georgia	Guatemala
Haiti	Honduras	Indonesia
Jamaica	Jordan	Latvia
Liberia	Lithuania	Moldova
Mongolia	Mozambique	Nauru (Island in the South Pacific)
Netherlands	Nicaragua	Niger
Nigeria	North Korea	Panama
Paraguay	Peru	Philippines
Romania	South Africa	Sudan
Tajikistan	Trinidad	Ukraine
United States	Zambia	

APPENDIX 3
CHARITIES WATCHDOG

T he following letter is from Trent Stamp, the Executive Director, Charity Navigator, a watchdog group for charities.

December 14, 2006

Dear Rick O'Dwyer:

On behalf of Charity Navigator, I wish to congratulate *Gleanings tor the Hungry* on achieving our coveted four-star rating for sound fiscal management.

As the nonprofit sector continues to grow

at an unprecedented pace, savvy donors are demanding more accountability, transparency, and quantifiable results from the charities they choose to support with their hard-earned dollars. In this competitive, philanthropic marketplace, Charity Navigator, America's premier charity evaluator, highlights the fine work of efficient charities such as your own, and provides donors with essential information needed to give them greater confidence in the charitable choices they make.

Based on the most recent financial information available, we have calculated a new rating for your organization. We are proud to announce Gleanings for the Hungry has earned our four-star rating for its ability to efficiently manage and grow its finances. Only twelve percent of the charities we've rated have received at least two consecutive four-star evaluations, indicating that Gleanings for the Hungry outperforms most charities in America in its efforts to operate in the most fiscally responsible way possible. This exceptional designation from Charity Navigator differentiates Gleanings for the Hungry from its peers and demonstrates to the public it is worthy of their trust.

The New York Times NPR and *The Chronicle of Philanthropy*, among others, have profiled and celebrated our unique method of applying data-driven analysis to the charitable sector.

We evaluate ten times more charities than our nearest competitor and currently attract more visitors to our website than all other charity rating groups combined; thus, making us the leading charity evaluator in America. Our irrefutable data shows that users of our site gave more than they planned to before viewing our findings, and in fact, last year Charity Navigator visitors gave over $3 billion in charitable gifts. Our favorable review of Gleanings for the Hungry's fiscal health will be visible on our website as of December 15.

Sincerely,

/ signed /

Trent Stamp

Executive Director

Charity Navigator

APPENDIX 4
ANGEL STORY

I have been to Gleanings for the Hungry several times. I have gone as both a youth leader and as a member of an adult team. This particular time I had come as part of a youth team from Lacey, Washington, under the leadership of Mark Schaufler. We had been there before and we had a great team of kids with us as usual. We had worked in the line and also laying fruit out for a couple of days, so we had the fruit-stained fingers and sticky clothes that processing fruit creates. The day was near end, and after our nightly devotions in the recreation room, our entire group was getting ready to settle into the girls and boys dorms for a night of much needed rest.

As it happened, I was waiting for the girls to finish their showers and head to the dorm, so I was wandering to and fro visiting with them, and encouraging them to get settled in. The boys were taking some time to get settled in their dorms. It was a very warm night; I can remember the smell of the sulfur from the sulfur houses and the sweet smell of fruit still clinging to our t-shirts and shorts as we waited for our turn in the showers. There were still several boys waiting outside the shower area and I struck up a conversation with Zach Lucas, one of our teens who visited with everyone and was very well liked by all. Zach had a zeal for life and a real heart for God — he worked hard at Gleanings, and usually had the biggest smile as we worked as a group. Our goal this year was to fill a semi-truck trailer with those white five-gallon buckets of dried fruit. We were well on our way to accomplishing our goal.

Zach and I were talking about how warm it was and how satisfying it was to see the rows and rows of pallets laden with fruit laying stretched out in the fields. We had worked together for quite a while that day unloading fruit trays onto the field, and were feeling pretty great about how much all our team had processed. We walked out towards the edge of the concrete slab next to the sulfur houses and looked out over the field.

Zach was talking to me, so I was facing him more than the field, as he was an animated talker, expressing himself with his hands in wide gestures. He was visiting with me about his dreams for the future. He had a desire to do great things for God and make a difference with his life.

Suddenly Zach stopped talking and his jaw dropped open. He pointed over my shoulder towards the field behind me and a look of fear and delight all mixed together came over his face. He began to sort of hop about, never taking his eyes off the field behind me. To tell you the truth I was a bit fearful at that point! I thought Zach had breathed in a bit too much sulfur!

Zach said "Look, Look, LOOK! Do you see what I see? Is that real? Look at that!"

I thought to myself, "My goodness, what is he so scared of?" and I was very reluctant to turn around. "Zach", I said, "What is it? What is wrong? Zach? Zach? Zach, STOP! What IS it?" But Zach was speechless, he just kept pointing and he began to laugh, but there were tears rolling down his cheeks.

My heart was beating wildly with fear, but I forced myself to turn and look at the field. Since we were in the light cast by the building's floodlights, it took a moment for my eyes to focus. Zach reached out and took my forearm, continuing to jump, laugh and cry all the while. As my eyes focused on the far end of the field, I rubbed them a little. Zach kept asking me, "Do you see that?" I thought at first that it was some kind of low fog out there. But there seemed to be some kind of form to the fog. I stepped a bit closer to the edge of the concrete and looked across the field from one end to the other at the fruit, and noticed again; something seemed to tell me something/someone was there. I turned and looked at Zach, then looked back at the field.

It was as if someone cleared my vision, like when you wipe a mirror with a soft cloth after it's been fogged up. I saw then what Zach had been looking at. There were angels in the field. They stood side by side, and while they did not look like flesh and blood, they were clearly there. To me they looked maybe eight to ten feet tall. They stood with a spear in one hand, elbows bent and hands nearly touching their middles, shoulder to shoulder; well, more like elbow to elbow. Their feet were shoulder width apart and I got the distinct feeling they were well-planted right where they were. They had no *face*, yet I knew they were facing me. They had on pointed-top helmets, and their chests had a shield-like appearance. The biggest impression I got from what I saw was incredible strength and protection, but I did not feel threatened in any way by what I saw. I began to cry and laugh like Zach and I looked at him in total disbelief. "Do you see it Cheryl? Do you see it?" Zach cried. I nodded my head and turned back to see the angels again.

It was then that I noticed they encircled the field and I knew immediately that they circled the entire compound. How I knew it, I do not know, but I was instantly sure of it. Zach still had my arm, and I pulled it away and grasped his arm then.

I began singing one of my favorite choruses, "This is Holy ground, we're standing on Holy ground...." and Zach joined in with me. Then we went right on to sing "We are standing on Holy ground, and I know that there are angels all around...." Somehow it felt like it was exactly what we were supposed to do at exactly that moment.

I did not want to move, nor did Zach, but we kept telling each other, "We need to go get Pastor Mark" and I am not sure about how Zach felt, but I had enough fear in me I didn't want him to leave me and go get Mark, and I didn't want to leave him to go either! Mostly I was afraid that if we left, we'd never see those angels again. I am not really sure how long we were out there looking at the angels, but I would guess close to an hour. Zach kept laughing and crying, and so did I. We'd start to back away towards the buildings, but then go back to the edge of the concrete.

Finally, we stepped back and talked. "I'm going to go get Mark!" Zach said. I knew by now that Zach and I were probably the only two left awake, and I could only imagine the uproar we would create if we started waking people up to talk about seeing angels, so I told him to wait until morning. I thought to myself – I hope Mark won't be mad at me for not waking him, but I am hardly believing this myself!" We walked towards the dorms, then walked back out to the edge of the concrete again. I couldn't see the angels anymore, but I knew in my heart they were still there.

Zach looked across the field, and seeing nothing either, said, "Did I imagine all that? Was I just looking at the trees out there and seeing things in a weird light?"

I thought for a moment, "Well, I thought I saw angels, but maybe I didn't," but inside I knew that what I saw was real and it was definitely out there. "No, Zach, you did not imagine it. We saw angels!"

"Zach," I said, "We have got to go to bed. We have a lot of work to do tomorrow!" We went to our separate areas, and I crawled onto my bunk, un-showered and sticky with fruit, and laid there and thought of what I had just experienced. I thought of something I'd heard several times—angels appeared over and over as recorded in the Bible, and they almost always said "Be not afraid" or "Fear not!" I understood why they said that now.

I took a long time to calm myself and drift off to sleep. I lay there for a very long time, half expecting a troop of angels to come dancing through the dorm at any moment, but I finally fell into a deep sleep.

The morning arrived sunny and warm and I was only up a few moments when Mark came to me and asked me to tell him what I had seen the night before. Zach had told him and he wanted to know what I saw. I relayed to Mark what I saw and he got the biggest grin and joy filled his face. He went to see Wally Wenge.

A short time later Mark returned to me and shared with me what happened when he shared my and Zach's story with Wally. As I remember it, the Gleanings staff had been praying that God would *place a hedge of angels around the compound.* Our vision was confirmation for them.

Our vision of the angels blessed Zach and I. For me, it confirmed that God is real and He loves all of us enough to meet our needs. For the staff of Gleanings for the Hungry, it confirmed God was in their midst and answering their prayers.

Needless to say, that night there were seventy-five plus students and leaders standing at the edge of that concrete at bedtime, but God had already completed what He wanted to accomplish for the staff of Gleaning for the Hungry. They knew He was with them.

Over the years I have not always been perfect with my choices, but I am grateful that God is allowing me to be used in the ministry that I most love. Zach, I hear, is in full-time ministry and Mark has since travelled worldwide as an evangelist and writer. Gleanings will always hold a very special place in my heart and I am thankful for the blessings I've received while there. I know God uses this ministry world-wide and I am thankful to have been a worker in the field.

Cheryl Rasmussen
Declo, ID
May 2005

APPENDIX 5
TESTIMONIES

Again Jesus said, "Simon son of John, do you truly love me?" He answered, "Yes, Lord, you know that I love you." Jesus said, "Take care of my sheep." The third time he said to him, "Simon son of John, do you love me?" Peter was hurt because Jesus asked him the third time, "Do you love me?" He said, "Lord, you know all things; you know that I love you." Jesus said, "Feed my sheep. John 21.16-17

In the beginning of our ministry, I was invited to speak at three different churches on the same Sunday morning. At first, very early in the morning, the pastor preached briefly on John 21, exactly the same passage that I had chosen for my first talks. What a coincidence, I thought. After a brief stop for coffee and hugs, I drove quickly to a mid-morning service at church number two. The pastor there chose John 21 for his introduction of our ministry. I remember remarking on the significance of this happening twice. These pastors had not spoken to one another or to me regarding their choice of scripture passage for this day's message.

Immediately following my talk, I excused myself and drove much too fast, in order to arrive in time to speak to the third and final church congregation. This was a small church, pastored by an old friend who was well into his sermon on the book of John, Chapter 21, "Feed my sheep."

I was nearly overcome to speak. When I began, I showed my old friend my notes. He wrapped a long robed arm around my shoulders and said, "Well, friends, I guess we're going to be feeding some sheep." And so we have.

For nearly twelve years now we have been feeding hungry children and their families in and around the small city of Linjlang, Jilin Province, PRC. The weather there is brutal, the government oppressive and highly suspicious of foreigners, the church dominated and fearful, much of the population desperately poor. Every day we work to feed the hungry, to provide education, medical help, and by demonstrating the love of our Lord, provide a positive role model for a government system so corrupt that even those who would like to help feel helpless. We are not helpless. Like a beacon in the dark, God shows us how to help these people. We do not work alone. He has provided generous benefactors who give sacrificially to carry on His work in this very remote and forlorn piece of earth. One of the largest of our providers is Gleanings for the Hungry.

Twice they have given a full container of food, each weighing approximately 44,000 pounds. Huge buckets filled with golden peaches and nectarines, dried in the

California sun, oatmeal, soup, dried beans, raisins, a bounty of riches to little children and their families who have been eating nothing but dried corn and wild celery. When the huge truck pulls up to the bridge to our orphanage to unload, crowds begin to gather and hundreds of people watch in awe. The buckets and boxes that come out of the truck take over two hours to unload... such an unbelievable gift. Free food. "Why?" "Who brought it?" "Who is it for?" "The government?' "No."

In the beginning the government tried to take credit for the gift. The people soon figured it out. This is not given by any government, but by loving friends from America. When they ask us "why?" We simply say that our faith teaches us to love our neighbors as ourselves. A loving neighbor would never let his friend starve. We are a friend and neighbor and we live our life according to our faith. We plant seeds carefully always walking a fine line between bold witness and extreme caution. Often interrogated and threatened by the local security police and closely watched, our generosity, gifts of food, helps, compassion, constancy, and love are our primary witness. We wear a cross, purchased in China, around our necks. We pray for every family who receives our help. Rumor has it that if you are sick and eat our food, you will become well. Not surprising.

How to measure the effectiveness of our witness there? We will never know, nor do we need to. We are called to be faithful to scatter the seeds now, to deliver the food provided by sweating young bodies in the hot California sun, accept and partner with shippers who donate discounted space on cargo ships, foundations that send financial provision, administrators who make endless calls and write endless letters of request, prayers who pray. Perhaps one day we will see a harvest. All in God's good time. Today, we help to till the soil and pray that the seeds we are entrusted with will one day bear healthy fruit.

Cindy Reynolds, Threshold Ministries,

Linjiang, Jilin Province, PRC, March 27, 2007

For almost twenty years, the Foundation For His Ministry has received generous donations of food products for the destitute. We are always grateful for these contributions such as dried fruit, soup base and other items that you have given for the mission/orphanage in Baja California, Mexico. The dried fruit is a blessing to staff and children.

The Outreach Ministry to the poorest of the poor in the migrant work camps was also delighted when they received food that could be distributed. Every week our child evangelists go to the camps, teaching the children Bible stories, and distributing a cup of milk, a scoop of peanut butter, and dried fruit from Gleanings for the Hungry. Over 2,000 children are being reached through this vital program.

The dried vegetables are used for a soup base, which is served in the mission soup kitchen. Over 1,000 people each month are served in this discipleship center. Many make a decision to receive Christ.

Recently a visiting dentist wrote about his concern for

giving out too much candy to the children. Gleanings gave us a referral and we received 2,000 pounds of honey-glazed sunflower seeds. This was an answer to our prayers for providing a nutritious treat and snack especially for the children in our outreach program.

This is not the first time that Gleanings has provided more than what we could even imagine or hope — because of this, we see God is at work. And because of these gifts, people who have little or no hope are blessed, and they believe. In this one story, thousands of lives will be touched — the dentist and other visitors who have concern for the welfare of these children, our office who looks to fill the needs, and all the children who will receive the seeds.

Thank you for your work and for caring for the needs of those who are hungry.

Charla Pereau,

Foundation For His Ministry, Baja California, Mexico

March 26, 2007

reetings in the strong name of Jesus from Mongolia, the Land of Blue Sky! For many years my ministry has been blessed by Gleanings for the Hungry. Many of you lift us in your prayers. Some have given financial support to Gleanings designated to assist our efforts in Mongolia. But all of you who volunteer at Gleanings for the Hungry give us a gift of great impact that you don't even think of.

Those of you who volunteer your time and energies

give us a gift of life. Yes, the hard work of your hands, the sweat of your brow, there in the orchards of California, means life to so many here in Mongolia.

My brothers and sisters, your toil is literally saving lives here in Mongolia. Babies, children, teens, and adult lives are being saved and the Gospel of Jesus Christ is being preached to them. Your efforts in California are being blessed and multiplied by God here in Mongolia. He is using you to reach people with life-saving and life-sustaining gifts of food. That food is opening doors for witness and God's Holy Spirit is moving across this land.

In the past six years, with the assistance of Gleanings for the Hungry and all those who volunteer, we have provided food to over 30,000 individuals and families. Always remember that God is using YOU to bless people all around the world. Be mindful that even though you may never meet me, my wife Susan, or any of the children or adults we serve in Mongolia while we trod this earth, there will be a day when we will all rejoice around God's Throne in Heaven.

Thank you so much for serving us through your volunteer efforts at Gleanings for the Hungry. May God bless all of you.

Jerry Smith, President

CTW Life Qwest, Mongolia

June 6, 2006

For the past eight years the Armenian Gospel Mission has been the grateful recipient of quality food products from Gleanings for the Hungry. As I write, there are two forty-foot containers of raisins, dried fruit, wheat flour, and packaged oats destined for Armenia that will be consumed by several thousand impoverished children, families, and elderly in the Republic of Armenia and in Nogorno-Karabagh, formerly occupied by Azerbaijan.

Our programs in these regions are not only humanitarian in nature, they are ministering to the spiritual needs of two thousand children in seventeen Armenian Gospel Mission (AGM) schools as well as family members of the children who frequently receive Gospel literature and Bibles and are encouraged to attend Evangelical churches.

During the past year, AGM and the Armenian Relief and Development Agency (ARDA) Health Center in northern Armenia have been able to bring hope to 6,700 patients who receive medical assistance as well as nutritional supplements and food. Additionally, patients are invited to a growing home Bible fellowship where more than 100 patients and family members have been attending weekly services.

The ARDA Home Health program is a new and effective ministry for homebound, poverty-stricken individuals in families that lack the resources to meet their basic human needs. At present, 227 families receive medical and nutritional assistance by a staff medical doctor and social worker who minister with Christian love and compassion.

The generous assistance provided by Gleanings for the Hungry has been a source of great blessing for the Armenian Gospel Mission and its ministries in Armenia.

Steve Lazarian, President

Armenian Gospel Mission, Inc.

April 3, 2007

⌒⌒

In the containers that you sent to Moldova, we received dried fruits, raisins, and dried soup. The goods were distributed to orphanages, the elderly, impoverished families, and handicapped individuals. What a blessing you have been and continue to be for those who are in need in the Republic of Moldova.

All the food items were such a blessing for so many in Moldova. The best words of gratitude come directly from those who benefited from your generosity. For this reason, we have included excerpts from the hundreds of letters of gratitude we received at the Little Samaritan Mission headquarters in Chisinau.

Victor - an eleven year old from Visoca Orphanage, Moldova:

> I am an orphan. There are 120 orphans just like me in our orphanage/school. We live in an orphanage in the northern part of Moldova where it is colder than in the southern part of Moldova. Fruits such as apples and cherries grow in this part of Moldova, but we don't have peaches and grapes because it is too cold.

We don't taste these fruits at all. But God is so good to us and He loves us so much. He takes care of us always. Our Lord sent us raisins and dried peaches from across the ocean from the United States. Now we know what they taste like and we can have "compot" (dried fruits boiled in water) and it is like a juice from the dried fruits and raisins. It's the best juice we ever had. Also, we received sweet rolls with raisins for a snack. You should see how the smaller kids break the roll and eat the raisins first from the bread rolls, and then they eat the rolls. I wish you could visit us at lunch or dinnertime to see our joy. Thank you for taking care of us.

Lilian Turcanu — sixth grade — Drochia Orphanage, Moldova:

I always pray before and after the meal, but after eating porridge for breakfast, lunch, and dinner for so long, we would like to taste something else. But what can we do? We eat what we have. One day the school bus left and, after a short time, it came back with food from Gleanings for the Hungry. We were so excited because we knew that we would eat something tasty and different from what we eat every day. We really missed the dried fruit and soups. But our joy was even greater when for breakfast we received a bar that tasted like chocolate. We know that these are from Gleanings for the Hungry because only from there do we receive such tasty chocolate and dried fruit. Now, even our daily porridge became more appetizing, because it had raisins in it. We were told how these fruits are dried in the hot sun there in California and we want to give thanks to the people who worked and made it possible for us to eat such delicacies. May God bless you and give you strength so that you can be able to send us more often, if it is possible, such good things.

Little Samaritan Mission, Inc.

Hickory, North Carolina 28603

January 9, 2008

The donation from Gleanings for the Hungry was incredibly effective in providing high protein snacks for individuals who were drastically affected by Hurricane Katrina. Food was provided through our distribution sites as individuals and families came forward to receive aid. We were also able to go door-to-door praying with people, providing assistance to re-roof their homes, cut down their fallen trees, and give them a listening ear. Your donation was a wonderful assistance to our efforts by providing nourishment for victims as well as relief workers.

Organization: Friendships,

Hurricane Katrina Relief

Fifty children in Mamoli, Southern Mozambique, were unschooled, homeless orphans before Simao and Annette Mucache arrived. They have taken in these children and provided accommodation and schooling where there are no roads, no electricity, no running water. They have to feed these children three times daily and do it completely by faith. The food you sent is so precious to them. To be there as they give thanks and praise God is very heartrending.

All of our seventy-five plus missionaries who distribute the food in their area are people who love the poor and suffering and are overwhelmed by your enabling them to bless people as they preach the gospel.

Simon and Annette Mucache, Mamoli

Southern Mozambique

The donation of raisins provided by Gleanings for the Hungry added an essential ingredient to the bread produced at our bakery in North Korea. North Korean children do not usually have the opportunity to eat fruit or any sources of sugar, so the addition of raisins to our bread became a very special feature of our bakery and a major service to the children of that region. Because of the raisin donation, our bread is renowned throughout the city for being the most delicious.

Though it is usually impossible to share the Gospel verbally with someone in North Korea because of the security risks, we are able to live out a daily testimony of our Lord and Savior through the special care we give our North Korean employees and the entire community around our bakery. In a country where everyone lives only for themselves and citizens cannot even trust their own spouses, every North Korean involved in our projects knows that they can trust us and sees how we voluntarily devote ourselves to improving their country and giving hope to their people without any personal gain for ourselves. Though they are taught from childhood to despise foreigners and disdain the outside world, they see us helping and providing for them when their government only makes empty promises and lets them starve. This is the greatest testimony we can give.

We are not usually allowed to talk to the students who receive our bread; however, the testimony is seeing how happy they are to receive it and how quickly they consume it. On one occasion a homeless child in rags approached our vehicle begging for money. Fortunately we had some of the bread with us and were able to give him a couple of buns which he quickly snatched out of our hands and held tightly like a treasure. As quickly as he could without being noticed, for fear that someone would take it away from him, he ran around the corner and as we drove by we saw him furiously devouring the bread as fast as he could get it into his mouth. It was such a touching sight to see this malnourished child enjoying our bread, containing the donated raisins, that it moved me to tears and it is a moment I will never forget.

Aaron Valdizan, TRADI Program Officer

North Korea

The donation from Gleanings for the Hungry of cereal, red beans, raisins, rice, and yellow corn was a tremendous blessing for our people. There were people who came a distance of about six miles who benefited. Many people who witnessed the distribution commented on the thoughtfulness and exemplary work being done by our church. The outreach was such a success and the donation of food, especially the red beans, rice, and raisins, was on the front page of Kingston's biggest newspaper. Many people were helped and many people heard the salvation message. Thanks to the food and work of our volunteers, over 1,000 people put their faith in Christ.

Life Assembly of God, Kingston, Jamaica

ABOUT THE AUTHOR

Steve spent his teen years in the rough and tumble ranchlands of Northern British Columbia. After Steve and Becky married in 1975, they spent an amazing, fifteen-month "honeymoon" in a tiny log cabin in the Canadian Rockies. Surrounded by majestic mountains, untouched wilderness, and marvelous solitude, they began their new life of adventure together.

The North of Canada is a unique and rich cultural landscape. The harsh natural environment forces you to learn a variety of skills. Steve's early vocational list reads a bit like a shopping list! He was farmer, logger, trapper, tree planter, fire fighter, carpenter, and first aid attendant.

Then in their late twenties, Steve and Becky packed a few belongings and their two young children, Heather and Shannon, and took the step of faith to join Youth With A Mission. It was during this four and one half year season that they were honored to meet and serve alongside Wally and Norma Wenge and the fledgling ministry called Gleanings for the Hungry.

It was during their seasons of service at Gleanings that they attended a local church called Wellspring Christian Center. They felt very at home there, making fast friends with Pastor Doug Hagey and many of the congregants. What a surprise it was to receive the call to join the pastoral staff at Wellspring. Saying yes meant a permanent move to Dinuba, California, and a decade of blessed ministry and lifelong friendship.

The approach of a new millennia, meant a transition in life and ministry. Sent out by the Wellspring Congregation, as missionaries to Canada, Steve and Becky returned once again to Northern British Columbia. Serving as the Foursquare Church Supervisor for Northwestern Canada, Steve traveled extensively.

Currently serving as Senior Pastor of the multiethnic congregation of Bible Fellowship Foursquare Church, Steve continues his role as Supervisor.

The author's association with Gleanings for the Hungry began in 1986 and has continued to the present. Annually accompanying bus loads of youthful volunteers, Steve has been privileged to see all the miraculous and remarkable changes. Today, Steve serves as a member of the Gleanings Board of Directors in the role of Secretary/Treasurer.

Steve and Becky have enjoyed thirty-two wonderful years of marriage. Their two lovely daughters are married and have graced their lives with the treasure of four beautiful grandchildren.

Steve Witmer
Senior Pastor, Bible Fellowship
Surrey, BC

CPSIA information can be obtained at www.ICGtesting.com
Printed in the USA
BVOW02s1240280314

348990BV00001B/3/P